# The Santa Cruz Ghost Directory

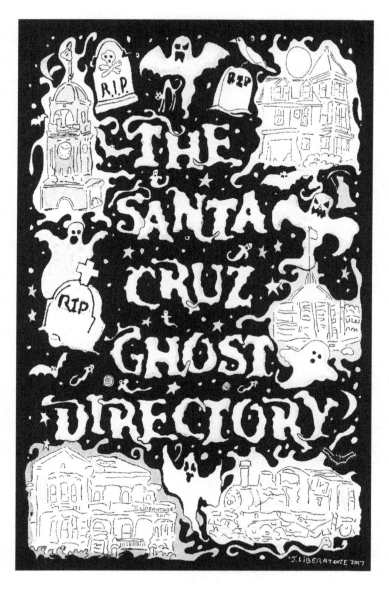

# Aubrey Graves

Copyright © 2018: Aubrey Graves
All rights reserved.
*Santa Cruz Ghost Directory, The* ©
ISBN-13: 978-1544959320
ISBN-10: 154495932X
Graves, Aubrey
Photos by: Aubrey Graves (Unless otherwise noted)
Illustrated by: John Liberatore

# DEADication

Dedicated to all the lost souls of Santa Cruz ...
may you one day find peace.

*Photoshoped image of the notorious White Lady of Santa Cruz at her former home, by Aubrey Graves*

# TABLE OF CONTENTS

**INTRODUCTION** .......................................... 13

**THE OHLONE INDIANS** ............................... 15

**APTOS**

The Bayview Hotel ......................................... 22

Forest of Nisene Marks ................................. 27

Sea Breeze Tavern ......................................... 28

**BEN LOMOND**

Love Creek Road ............................................ 30

Mountain Community Theater ..................... 32

**BOULDER CREEK**

Boulder Creek Cemetery ............................... 34

Joe's Bar ........................................................ 35

The White Cockade ....................................... 38

## BROOKDALE

The Brookdale Lodge .................................. 40

## CAPITOLA

Cinelux ....................................................... 49
The Shadowbrook ...................................... 51
The Rispin Mansion ................................... 54

## DAVENPORT

Saint Vincent DePaul Church ..................... 58
Waddell Creek ............................................ 59

## FELTON

The Cremer House ..................................... 60
East Zayante Road ..................................... 63
Felton Cemetery ......................................... 64
Lompico Mountain ..................................... 66
Monty's Log Cabin ..................................... 67
Roaring Camp Railroads ............................ 71

**SANTA CRUZ**

Arana Gulch ................................................. 76
The Asti ....................................................... 79
The Boardwalk Bowl ..................................... 81
Bocci's Cellar ............................................... 82
Callahan's Pub ............................................. 86
The Catalyst ................................................. 89
Cliff Crest Bed and Breakfast ....................... 93
Coffeetopia .................................................. 95
The Del Mar Theater .................................... 97
Dominican Hospital ..................................... 98
Evergreen Cemetery .................................. 102
The Golden Gate Villa ............................... 105
Holy Cross Cemetery ................................. 109
Highway 17 ............................................... 113
Jeffery's Restaurant .................................. 115
The Jury Room .......................................... 116
Mark Abbott Memorial Lighthouse ............. 120
Mission Santa Cruz ................................... 121
The Mystery Spot ...................................... 126
Paradise Park ............................................ 129

| | |
|---|---|
| Pogonip | 132 |
| Pono Hawaiian Grill | 135 |
| Railroad Tracks | 137 |
| The Red Room | 138 |
| Sake – Japanese Steakhouse and Sushi | 142 |
| The San Lorenzo River | 144 |
| Santa Cruz Beaches | 146 |
| Santa Cruz Beach Boardwalk | 147 |
| Santa Cruz Memorial | 157 |
| Santa Cruz Mountain Tunnels | 160 |
| Santa Cruz Museum of Art and History | 164 |
| The Sunshine Villa | 166 |
| Surf Bistro and Bakery | 170 |
| Red, White, and Blue Beach | 171 |
| University of California, Santa Cruz | 176 |
| Walnut Avenue | 181 |
| Water Street Bridge | 184 |
| The West Cliff Inn | 186 |
| White Lady's | 189 |
| Wilder Ranch | 197 |

## SCOTTS VALLEY

Alfred Hitchcock's Late Estate .................... 201

Bruno's BBQ .............................................. 208

Cinelux ..................................................... 211

## SOQUEL

Blue Ball Park ........................................... 214

The Daubenbiss House .............................. 214

The Soquel Cemetery ................................ 218

## WATSONVILLE

Hecker Pass .............................................. 219

Mount Madonna County Park .................... 221

Lee Road .................................................. 225

The Redman House ................................... 226

The Tuttle Mansion ................................... 229

Veteran's Memorial Building ...................... 230

## MORE HAUNTS .......................................... 233

## GLOSSARY ................................................ 239

*Evergreen Cemetery, Santa Cruz*

## INTRODUCTION

Originated in 1850, Santa Cruz County is known for its dark historic past and its thin veil to other dimensions. Many spirits are said to dwell in the county, tarrying with a different motive for each one. Famous psychic Sylvia Browne (RIP) believes Santa Cruz has so much paranormal activity because of the all the moisture in the air, making it more of a comfortable climate for ghosts to reside. No one really knows why each spirit is staying near our plane of existence, yet we can be aware of the reality that they are all around us.

All of the hauntings and ghost stories being told around Santa Cruz County have inspired me to investigate these allegations. Join me as I share both legends and true encounters, as we venture into the world of the unknown...

## THE OHLONE INDIANS

*A painted mural of the Ohlone Indians, date and artist unknown*

The Ohlone Indians settled on California's central coast around 10,000 B.C.E. The local tribe, known as the Awaswas, was known to live throughout Santa Cruz County and spoke a variety of different languages. The Ohlones, also known as Costanoans, were very spiritual, and had several supernatural and mythological stories that they told. Unfortunately, the majority of the tales were lost over time, and only a few remain.

One of the oldest spooky legends of Santa Cruz told by the Ohlone Indians was the story of the Sycamore Grove Spider. It was claimed by the Native Americans that the flat area from Highway 9 to the San Lorenzo River was cursed and inhabited by a giant supernatural spider. The creature lived in the dark and uncanny grove, feeding off of humans, with bad intentions. The Ohlone Indians believed that the people who hid darkness in their souls, and passed by the area would get tangled in the mystical spider's web; and be trapped for all eternity. Some tribe members said they saw the enormous web, "jeweled by dew drops from the fog, deep in the woods." Witnesses reported seeing stolen souls wander the area. This legend carried throughout history, is still told by a few locals today, who say that spirits killed by the supernatural spider still haunt the Sycamore Grove.

*The Santa Cruz Ghost Directory*

The Native Americans lived through many hardships, and dealt with enemies from time to time, particularly after the white man took over.

Rumor has it, long ago a tragic event took place near River Street and Mission, and the residual energy from it still lingers. The Ohlones were attacked by another tribe and many lives were taken. A local Indian woman claimed that after the attack, bones covered the area so thoroughly that one couldn't even walk without stepping on them. Since the battle, it has been observed that over 20 strange deaths have been accounted for in the area; some believe it has to do with the bad juju that occurred on the land.

The Ohlones had very strong spiritual beliefs about being buried properly. They had several sacred burial spots around the county that were kept undisturbed and untouched. They believed that if their grave was disturbed (such as being moved, or covered by buildings and roads, etc.) that they would no longer be able to rest. As the Ohlone population decreased, their burial spots were slowly forgotten. Most of the sacred burial grounds have been desecrated, and built over; which could contribute to the hauntings and curses around Santa Cruz County.

Former burial grounds are still being discovered around the county. The most well-known burial sites are along Lee Road in Watsonville, Mission Park, and beneath houses on Beach Hill, in Santa Cruz. In 1908, another scared burial ground was found in Davenport, Santa Cruz. Without any thought or respect, the bones were removed from the land and taken away. Depot Hill at "Lover's Lane" in Capitola could also be a former sacred burial ground, according to Santa Cruz historian Margaret

Koch. In the 1960s, the skeletons of six Ohlone Indians were found buried along Depot Hill, as well as along the creek that runs through the Capitola Village.

Indian remains have also been found along the San Lorenzo River, at the end of Market Street, in backyards, under houses, and beneath the streets and sidewalks around the county. Who knows ... You might even have an Ohlone or two buried on your property.

*Ohlone Indian remains that were uncovered at an Aptos residence, Santa Cruz Sentinel, July 18, 1954*

*The Santa Cruz Ghost Directory*

# 28 Indian Skeletons are Unearthed at Davenport

*Santa Cruz Weekly, January 11, 1908*

# GRUESOME FIND UNEARTHED ON BEACH HILL

## The Remains of an Indian Dug up Saturday Morning by Milo Du Pee

*Santa Cruz Weekly, June 28, 1908*

Spirits of the Awaswas tribe have been heard and sighted throughout Santa Cruz County for centuries. Mission Santa Cruz is claimed to have several of their souls lingering.

*The Santa Cruz Ghost Directory*

*Ohlone Indians, artwork by unknown, public domain*

Pogonip Park is also said to be inhabited by the spirits of Indians, and burdened by an old Ohlone curse.

Ghosts of the Native Americans have been seen by commuters along scenic roads during the hours of darkness.

On Highway 17, as well as on Lee Road in Watsonville, the spirit of an old Indian man has been sighted traveling on foot.

# APTOS

### The Bayview Hotel

*Circa 1900, courtesy of the Bayview Hotel*

The gallant Bayview Hotel was built in 1878 and still stands on Soquel Drive in the cute, quaint Aptos Village. The oldest hotel in Santa Cruz County was built by a pioneer man by the name of Joseph Arano. The Santa Cruz local and his family ran the hotel until his tragic death in 1928. In the evening of September 21, 1928, a fire started in the west wing of the hotel, which killed Arano in his sleep at 91 years of age.

## APTOS RESIDENTS MOURN DEATH OF JOSEPH E. ARANO, PIONEER CITIZEN AND FIRST MERCHANT

*Santa Cruz Evening News, September 29, 1928*

The amazing 12-room Victorian structure has been visited by many famous, prominent people, including Lillian Russell, and King Kalakaua of Hawaii.

*The Santa Cruz Ghost Directory*

It is alleged that in 1868, hundreds of people who died of Smallpox in the area were buried and covered in lime in one mass grave located right behind the Bayview Hotel, (in the empty lot) and are still there today.

For more than a century, spirits have roamed this hotel, making their presence known by creating an abundance of disturbances with their enigmatic energies. Some customers will actually up and leave in the middle of the night because they are scared out of their wits.

# Ghosts said to haunt hotel

*Santa Cruz Sentinel, October 31, 1986*

All staff members, as well as the current owner and her two daughters have had numerous accounts of paranormal experiences. Ghosts residing at the hotel are known to turn computers and televisions on and off, and change channels right in front of viewers. Many have heard footsteps, as well as disembodied voices, and singing in the halls.

Reports of sightings include the ghost a little boy, who has been seen looking out the windows, and is said to be heard knocking on doors. A spirit of a woman has also been seen in the downstairs bathroom with a child.

In 2013, I spoke with Christina, the Bayview's current owner since 2002, who affirms that the Hotel is indeed haunted. It would take her all day to explain all of her encounters with the ghosts who reside there. Christina's first experience was on her very first night in the hotel. She felt a cold gust of wind, and then smelled the scent of roses. Christina turned to where she felt the breeze in the hallway and saw the apparition of a woman standing on the other side of the mirror. Christina's bed would also shake violently right before she would go to sleep . . . every night for six months.

Christina and her daughters live on the third story of the hotel. They believe that visitors from the past must have passed away on the top floor, possibly the past owner who allegedly died there long ago. I asked Christina where the most paranormal occurrences happen and she verified that it is on the entire second level. The bar at the Bayview is known to have lots of paranormal activity as well.

Just before I had visited in 2013, Christina's daughter had taken a photo of her refection in the hall mirror. Upon reviewing the photo, she noticed a hand coming from the opposite side of the mirror pushing out from the glass.

From stirring apparitions and dark shadows to faces, orbs, moving objects, disembodied voices, eerie sounds, and its very own graveyard, this haunted hotel really has it all.

BAYVIEW HOTEL
Historical Landmark
Year built: 1878
8041 Soquel Drive
Aptos, CA 95003
(831) 688-8654

## The Forest of Nisene Marks

There are legends that long ago within the deep, dark forest of Nisene Marks witches who lived nearby were hung and killed for practicing witchcraft. According to local folklore, the ghosts of the witches have been seen by hikers hanging from the trees, their eyes pure black and filled with malevolence.

THE FOREST OF NISENE MARKS
Aptos Creek Road & Soquel Drive
Aptos, CA 95003

## The Sea Breeze Tavern

Known as "the local haunted house," overlooking Monterey Bay in the Rio Del Mar flats is said to be haunted by the bar's first owner, Georgia May Derber whose lonesome and untimely death occurred within the structure. On June 8th, 2004, Georgia's mummified body was found in her apartment above the bar on her kitchen floor, due to complications of cancer. Because of her reclusive behavior, her body was unnoticed for quite some time, until a Sheriff Deputy just happened to stop by.

*The Santa Cruz Ghost Directory*

**GEORGIA MAY DERBER**

In 2007, the tavern was refurbished and reopened keeping Georgia in mind. It is claimed that she never left the structure and that her ghost still haunts the vicinity.

SEA BREEZE TAVERN
Year built: 1927
101 Esplanade
Aptos, CA 95003

# BEN LOMOND

### Love Creek Road

A little past midnight on January 4, 1982, tragedy struck in The Ben Lomond Mountains. A massive landslide that was estimated to be 500 yards wide and 700 yards long crashed down on dozens of homes overlooking Love Creek Road. A witness recalled seeing "the trees snap like toothpicks" along with others who saw homes filled with mud, and cars completely buried with mud and trees, falling into the San Lorenzo River below.

The horrific mudslide ended up killing ten people. Some were never found.

A large memorial continues to sit about a mile up Love Creek Road, marking the area where two of the most remembered victim's rest. There, a sign reads:

*"Somewhere in this area lie my two grandsons, Trevor, 7 & Kelly, 5.*
*Please do not dump any trash. Grandma Olsen."*

The boy's bodies had been completely buried by the slide and they were never found. For years many visitors have come to pay their respects to the boys, leaving toys and trinkets at their grave site.

Locals and neighbors allege seeing the apparitions that didn't make it that tragic night wandering the area of Love Creek. Some believe the spirits are trying to uncover their lost bodies.

LOVE CREEK ROAD
Ben Lomond, CA 95005

## Mountain Community Theater

Once an old carriage house, the quaint mountain theater was first erected in 1923, by an old local pioneer by the name of Elisha Brooks.

For many years the haunted historic site has been used for plays, performances, and meetings and the residual energy lingers. While visiting the historic site I asked the theater's handyman if he had ever heard of the building being haunted.

"Oh, for sure!" he began. "One of the current employees has even said to have seen a ghost of an elderly man in the theater!"

"I even have experiences there I can't explain," he told me with sincerity. "Many times when I am there alone I hear noises and footsteps above me in the attic."

The handyman explained to me how he would go up to the attic to see if anyone was there, and there never is (or was).

MOUNTAIN COMMUNITY THEATER (PARK HALL)
Historical Landmark
Year built: 1923
9400 Mill Street
Ben Lomond, CA 95005
(831) 336-4777
https://mctshows.org/

# BOULDER CREEK

## Boulder Creek Cemetery

Established in 1862, the Boulder Creek Cemetery (I.O.O.F. Cemetery) has its share of paranormal activity. Dark shadow people have been seen meandering late at night in the eerie cemetery on occasion, EVPs have been caught, high EMF has been discovered, and rapid and drastic temperature fluctuations have been noticed.

*The Santa Cruz Ghost Directory*

BOULDER CREEK CEMETERY
(AKA I.O.O.F. Cemetery)
Year established: Circa 1862
Harman Street
Boulder Creek, CA 95006

**Joe's Bar**

Old deceased patrons still visit and, or occupy their favorite haunt at Joe's Bar in downtown Boulder Creek. I first found out about the spirits at Joe's while stopping in one day for a rare afternoon cocktail. As soon as I sat down at the bar, I felt spiritual energy and sensed something was watching me from the vicinity near the bathrooms.

"Is this place haunted?" I asked the bartender.

"I have heard it is ... by old customers," she said with a smile.

A few months later I went back to Joe's Bar and spoke to another bartender who knew a little more information.

"Have you gone into the basement here yet?" She asked me.

"No, I haven't," I replied. "Is that were one of the ghosts hangs out?"

"Yes," she said. "And it's creepy ... would you like to come see?" she asked.

"Oh yes please!" I said. "I'd love to, thanks."

As we began walking down the stairs into the dark basement I felt the energy get heavier and heavier. I began sensing a masculine energy that was annoyed that we were down there. The bartender pointed over to where the ghost is believed to hang out, which was directly below the vicinity near the bathrooms, where I had first sensed something upon arrival.

"Oh how funny," I began. "Right above that area upstairs is where I first felt him."

"Yeah, he's here." She announced.

"I'm not sure if he wants us down here though, it feels like he thinks we're invading his space," I shared.

As we walked back up the stairs I felt the energy get lighter with each step.

Whenever local psychic Shelly Crowley walks past Joe's Bar, she sees the ghosts of the old patrons from within the front window.

"There are always two or three ghosts there when I go by," Shelly shared with me.

JOE'S BAR
Year built: Early 1900s
13118 Highway 9
Boulder Creek, CA 95006
(831) 338-9417
www.joesbc.com

## The White Cockade

Deep in the woods of Boulder Creek sits the late White Cockade Scottish Pub. Built in 1930, the pub was known to be haunted by its first owner Barbara Stanford. This haunted pub was so eerie that some customers were known to come once and never go back again.

The latest owner claimed that one customer actually screamed in fright and ran out of the building after experiencing paranormal activity within the walls of the old hostelry. Many witnesses have said they saw Barbara's pale ghost in and around the pub when it was in operation.

In 2006, after her uncanny supernatural experience, Nancy Palajac was convinced that Barbara's spirit was trying to communicate. Nancy found the garland she had recently mounted on the floor with the tacks neatly stacked on a chair. Psychics say she's harmless and protective of the place, though she was known to be quiet the prankster. When there was an annoying customer at the pub, sometimes their bar stool would suddenly slip out from under them.

Additional Information:
-   Some say the Pub was being shared by ghosts. Another spirit that some believe reside there is the ghost a logger named Ben, who died in the 1980s.
-   Lights and stove burners were known to turn off and on by themselves.
-   Footsteps were heard in unoccupied rooms followed by Barbara Stanford's apparition.

THE WHITE COCKADE
Year built: 1930
(Closed since 2010)
18025 Highway 9
Boulder Creek, CA 95006

# BROOKDALE

### The Brookdale Lodge

Located in the deep, dark Santa Cruz Mountains stands the world-famous Brookdale Lodge, built in the early 1900s. It is said to be one of the most haunted locations in California.

The hotel is claimed by psychics and locals to be inhabited by 49 spirits, who decided to never check out. It is also believed that there are portals and vortexes around the lodge, allowing spirits to come and go as they please.

Being so outstanding and exceptional, with its creek which runs through the famous dining hall; many famous people have visited the Brookdale such as President Herbert Hoover,

*The Santa Cruz Ghost Directory*

James Dean, Marilyn Monroe, Mae West, Shirley Temple, Rita Hayworth, and many more.

From the 1920's to the 1940s, the lodge was home to many local gangsters, such as Al Capone. Legend has it that mafia members would bury bodies underneath the floors, and within secret tunnels, and passageways, leading to livid ghosts with bad intentions creating havoc around the hotel.

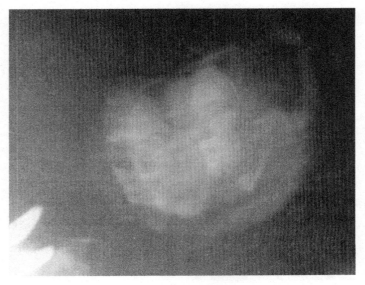

*Faces in the fire, Log Cabin Room fireplace, Brookdale Lodge. Photo by unknown, courtesy of Jane Reynolds Heath.*

Several hotel rooms are claimed to be occupied by spirits that scare some guests so badly, they leave without staying the night. Occupants have experienced unexplainable breezes and cold spots in their rooms, as well as strange sounds, noises, smells, electronic malfunctions, moving objects and ghostly vibes. Some claim to even have witnessed full body apparitions form before them, in addition to uncanny mists, and spirit orbs.

*The Brookdale Lodge, 2013*

*The Santa Cruz Ghost Directory*

*The Brookroom, Brookdale Lodge, 2013*

The Brookroom, built in 1922, is identified to have the most paranormal experiences throughout the hotel. Many have claimed to hear glasses, plates and silverware clinking, along

*The Santa Cruz Ghost Directory*

with footsteps, voices and even conversations from dozens of ghostly diners. Some have even caught spirits on film.

The Brookdale Lodge's first owner, Judge James Harvey Logan, is believed to haunt the vicinity. Psychics, including Sylvia Browne (RIP), claim to have made contact with him. After communicating with Logan, he allegedly slimed Browne with ectoplasm.

*Judge James Harvey Logan, circa 1900*

Legend has it, tragically, around the early 1900s, Judge James Harvey Logan lost his six-year-old niece, Sarah, while she was playing on the property one day and fell to her death in the creek that runs through the Brookroom. The little girl has been seen more than any other spirit in the lodge. Over the years, there have been countless sightings of her ghost, witnessed by visitors and employees alike. She is known to be seen in a blue and white Victorian-style Sunday dress near the fireplace in the lobby, running around the fireside room, playing in the brook, or throughout the halls; and on the balconies of the Brookroom. Some claim to have approached Sarah, speaking to her as she cried for her mother. When the eye witnesses look away, Sarah vanishes.

Another ghost who has been seen by many is speculated by psychics to be Sarah Logan's mother, or her nanny, Maria, who is believed to be looking for Sarah. This spirit is mostly seen in the Brookroom as well, standing on the front upper balcony. The smell of Gardenias often permeates the room at night, although there are no Gardenias throughout the haunted lodge. Several people who experienced the paranormal phenomenon assume that the smell is from the spirit from another time.

Residual sounds of big band music being played has been heard by guests and employees in the Band Room, as well as full-body apparitions being sited dancing on the dance floor.

The Mermaid Room is another hot spot in the lodge. Some have stated that they witnessed the ghost of a man standing at the bar having a drink long after closing. Visitors and employees have experienced hearing whispers, voices, clinking glasses, and soft music when the Mermaid Room was completely empty. The jukebox is known to turn off and on, and glasses and chairs move on their own.

The Pool Room is believed to be haunted by the thirteen-year-old girl who allegedly drowned in 1972, forcing the pool's closure. The long, browned-haired girl has been seen on occasion floating face down in the water or standing around in the Mermaid Room. Guests have complained about feeling cold spots randomly, in accompany with getting touched by unseen forces. Some say to have encountered hearing the teen speak quietly, and have seen splashing in the pool when it was vacant.

The Log Cabin, located off of the Brookroom was once used as the main entrance and lobby for the lodge for many years, and known as another hot spot of the hotel. A large, six-foot tall fireplace occupies one wall of the dark, rustic room where several paranormal investigators have had numerous experiences with the deceased. There are claims of objects moving on their own, seeing unexplainable mists, hearing and recording disembodied voices, and the feeling of an overwhelming sense of anxiety.

In the bar, there is usually some story going around about the most recent haunting. Bartenders at the Lodge are aware that they don't just clean up for the living; they clean up

*The Santa Cruz Ghost Directory*

after the dead as well, when glasses and bottles fly and slide off shelves.

One thing's for sure ... when asking for spirits at the Brookdale Lodge; you may just get more than a shot of whiskey.

THE BROOKDALE LODGE
Year built: 1903
11570 Hwy 9
Brookdale, CA 95007
(831) 609- 6010
https://brookdalelodge.com/

*For much more information and stories on the eerie lodge, check out my book, **The Haunted Brookdale Lodge**, available on Amazon.com.

# CAPITOLA

### Cinelux

Over the years, guests and staff have heard unexplainable sounds at the 41st Avenue movie theater, in addition to feeling as if they are being watched by an invisible force.

One night, years back while my friend was in the Ladies' Room, she felt as if someone was looking at her over the stall in the bathroom. Right after her unsettling experience, she asked an employee at the concession stand, "Is this place haunted?" The employee believed it was, and said that she also had something strange happen to her in a bathroom stall.

I interviewed former manager Chet Bauerle who had several unexplained encounters, particularly during the late hours of the night and after closing. "As closing manager, when you were there alone or with one other person, you always feel as if you're being watched, or that something was trying to help you. It wasn't necessarily friendly, but it also wasn't necessarily hostel. There are about five areas of the building that just feel off."

The former manager's most eerie encounter took place in Auditorium 1, while previewing movies after hours. While he was watching a film, he saw curtains near the exit sign begin to move. "The curtains would slightly move back and you'd see this figure look out," Chet explained. He said the ghost looked like an ethnic homeless person and wonders if maybe someone had gotten trapped and died in the vicinity long ago. His friend had also witnessed the figure standing near the exit on a different occasion, in addition to feeling the unsettling presence that lingers when the theater is practically empty. "I never went back into that auditorium unless there were other people in there," he stated.

Chet once saw the dark figure of a male standing in the hallway near Auditorium 3 after hours one night. It was there for only a second before it disappeared.

After interviewing Chet, he kindly gave me a short tour of the establishment. There I was able to feel exactly what he was talking about. That place definitely has a creepy vibe, especially in the projection booth. I spoke to another employee who is convinced that the projection booth is haunted. He said too many unexplainable things has happened to him up there, and you can just "feel it."

CINELUX
Year built: 1972
1475 41st Ave
Capitola, CA 95010
(831) 479-3504

**The Shadowbrook**

The mansion was first built for Ernestine O. Fowler, resident of San Francisco in the 1920s. It was used as his weekend getaway until 1940. The vacant quarters sat for five years before being bought, restored and remolded into the Shadowbrook, which opened its doors in 1947.

While the haunted house was unoccupied, many neighbors alleged seeing strange things along with having unusual and eerie experiences on the property. "...the presence of both a man and a woman have been seen," Randall A. Reinstedt, *California Ghost Notes*.

In recent years, apparitions and supernatural mists have been sighted in the enchanting restaurant during after-hours by former employees.

Objects are said to move on their o[wn]
as doors and windows that shut regularly
the air is still.

I spoke to an employee who said that he usually feels the presence of a male spirit while he's cleaning up on the bottom floor after closing for the night. The staff member alleged seeing napkins fly off the tables on their own occasionally. "I even saw it on the security camera one time," he stated.

A bartender shared with me that a guest had an unexplainable encounter late one evening in 2011 when she was in the ladies room. The young woman entered the powder room, thinking she was alone, but while she was in the stall, the lights suddenly turned off and she heard footsteps walking toward her. As the unseen force reached the door of her stall, the woman then heard shuffling which abruptly stopped. She opened the stall to find no one there. The experience left her with a chill.

One of the entities that has been sighted in the romantic and elegant establishment over the years just may be the friendly ghost of Fowler, who also haunts his old, charming estate.

SHADOWBROOK RESTAURANT
Year built: circa 1920s
1750 Warf Road
Capitola, CA 95010
(831) 475-1511
www.shadowbrook-capitola.com

## The Rispin Mansion

Built in 1921, the Rispin Mansion was first owned by the wealthy Rispin Family, then became a Monastary and later a training school. The mansion has abandoned, dilapidated, and condemned since the 1970s. Its lack of upkeep seems to incubate more paranormal occurrences from all its history. There are numerous spirits which haunt this eerie three-story building. Legend has it that anyone who lives there is cursed with losing all of their money.

The famous "Lady in Black," a Jesuit nun, makes her presence known more than any other ghost on the property. Several locals have experienced her paranormal antics, which include her full-body apparition appearing sporadically throughout the mansion. The nun has been observed standing in front of the top-story window looking down into the courtyard. She has also been witnessed reading a Bible in a rocking chair on the back porch. Some locals claim she has told visitors to, "Get out!"

Disembodied sounds of a dog barking and whining have been heard coming from the basement, also known as the dungeon. It is believed that this K-9 haunts the vincinty where he stayed when it was a police dog academy.

Back in the 1980s, after the house had been abandoned, a man allegedly fell through the floor boards three stories down to the basement. After crying for help for three days, he passed away from his injuries. Many have heard the spirit of a man cry out for help in the night. Other paranormal activity in the mansion includes hearing disembodied voices and screams, loud footsteps, windows and doors opening, as well as cold spots felt throughout this grandiose home. Some also attest to seeing the ghost of a man wearing glasses and holding a drink in front of the fireplace in the main room.

In October of 2012, my friends and I heard disembodied footsteps going down the cement pathway along the left side of the mansion late in the night. We kept waiting to see who was walking toward us, but no one was there. The footsteps continued off and on for minutes, and sometimes it sounded like multiple footsteps. Using a Mel Meter device we picked up random spikes around the perimeter of the mansion.

RISPIN MANSION
Historical Landmark
Year built: 1921
2200 Warf Road
Capitola, CA 95010
www.rispinmansion.com

# DAVENPORT

## Saint Vincent DePaul Church

According to author and paranormal investigator Jeff Dwyer, for generations, locals have witnessed apparitions coming and going from the Saint Vincent DePaul church. Some have observed anywhere from one to dozens of ghosts leaving the building at a time. Some who have seen this activity believe that the devoted religious spirits left some kind of imprints on the church, creating a residual haunting.

Sometimes they are seen in broad daylight, looking as if they are departing from a funeral or Sunday Worship. It is said that the ghosts are most often witnessed on gloomy, overcast mornings.

SAINT VINCENT DEPAUL CHURCH
Year built: 1915
123 Marine View Avenue
Davenport, CA 95017

### Waddell Creek

In 1875, a man by the name of William Waddell was walking through the forest on his land with his hunting dog when they got too close to a mama bear and her cub. The bear attacked Waddell and mangled his arm so severely that it had to be amputated, and was then buried in the north coast meadow.

Shortly after Waddell's passing, the mourners set off to unbury his limb for the funeral, but the arm had disappeared.

Ever since the arm's disappearance, people passing through Waddell Creek will mysteriously lose their belongings. Random items tend to go missing in the area, and Waddell's arm is always to blame. Stagecoach drivers would warn their passengers, while passing through the vicinity, to keep their possessions close and to watch out for "the sticky fingers of William Waddell's arm," according to a Metro Santa Cruz article in 1999.

WADDELL CREEK
Davenport, CA 95017

# FELTON

### The Cremer House

Built in 1876, the Cremer House, once known as "The Creamer Hotel" is the oldest building still standing in Felton, California. It was first built and opened by Thomas and Margaret Creamer as an 18-room hotel, gambling hall, and restaurant; which was said to once be harbored by contraband liquor and prostitutes. The Creamers both ran the boarding house until their deaths; Thomas passed in 1880, and Margaret in 1892.

At least 2 murders occurred at the old brothel over the years. First, in 1884, a man by the name of Win. Donnelly was found dead in is bed at the Cremer House, soon after he had been struck over the head with a fire poker by a contractor named George Jansey. Jansey owed money to Donnelly, and Donnelly was harassing him for it. As Donnelly was walking out of the Cremer House, he told Jansey, "I will murder you on site." Jansey then grabbed a fire poker near the hotel's stove and hit Donnelly over the head with it. Donnelly was said to have a couple drinks after he had been hit, then went to bed for his very last sleep at the Cremer House.

The second murder occurred in 1890, when two of the hotel's employees got into fight. The cook, George Duncan was stabbed to death by dishwasher, Henry Jackson.

Could these murder victims still be haunting the Cremer House? Locals, employees, and the current co-owner believe that the former hotel is haunted after experiencing a number of unexplainable events, particularly upstairs.

*Cremer House, 1940s*

According to a Monterey Bay article, Cremer House's co-owner Emily Thomas has been spooked on more than one occasion. There is even a tiny room upstairs that she refuses to enter because it scares her so much. Not only is eerie energy felt and sensed at times, but electrical malfunctions are said to happen frequently, as well as random and unexplainable cold spots in certain rooms.

"The women who do the filing back there have always noticed that when they're in there the light goes out," said Thomas. "We've had someone come in and change the light bulb, and someone come in and check the sockets and electrical in there, but every time they're in there the light will go out."

THE CREMER HOUSE
Year built: 1876
6256 Highway 9
Felton, CA 95018
(831) 335-3976
www.cremerhouse.com

**East Zayante Road**

One old legend of the valley is the ghost of an unknown horseman with a long overcoat who has been seen for generations along East Zayante Road. His full-body apparition has been sighted riding his ghostly steed particularly during twilight. Witnesses say he looked like he was from a different era. Many times when cars pass the haunted horseman he vanishes soon after.

EAST ZAYANTE ROAD
Felton, CA 95018


**Felton Cemetery**

The aged cemetery originated in the 1870s, and many of the graves are from that era. For the most part, the graveyard gives off a very welcoming and calm vibration, almost like being at Grandma's house. Though, there is one area, on the right side of the cemetery, where the energy is a little unsettling. High EMF has been found around the area, and possible spirit orbs have been caught on camera during the hours of darkness. Some of the spirits who dwell in the vicinity are open to communication. Disembodied footsteps have been heard, and cold spots felt. Some people have even claimed to have been touched by unseen forces.

One night, while my friend and I were investigating the cemetery, I asked the spirits if they could finish the last two knocks from the tune *Shave and a Haircut*. I knocked on the gazebo, waiting to hear the "two bits." Immediately, two uncanny knocks were heard.

While using the flashlight method to communicate with the spirits, one of them claimed to be an old soldier from World War II, and he seemed to be manipulating the light, possibly using Morse code.

"Are you using Morse code?" I asked.

The light stopped blinking and shined brightly.

In late 2012, I returned to the cemetery with psychic medium Jena Reece. During our visit, she saw the full-body apparition of a sailor dressed in a blue uniform standing just to the right of us several yards away. He stood there staring at us before vanishing. We approached the area where he had been, and sure enough, we found a grave marker for a young sailor.

FELTON CEMETERY
Year established: Circa 1870s
Love Street
Felton, CA 95018

**Lompico Mountain**

For many years the Ohlone Indians occupied Lompico, located in the deep, dark, Santa Cruz Mountains. Some residences claim that the Indian tribes left imprints on the land, and some are even said to still haunt it. On occasion, usually during sunset, and when the wind is right, it is said that you can actually hear the eerie beating of drums and ghostly chanting up on the mountain in certain areas.

LOMPICO MOUNTAIN
Year founded: 1927
Felton, CA 95018

**Monty's Log Cabin**

Every time I went past Monty's Log Cabin surrounded by tall redwoods along Highway 9, I always had a sense it was haunted. I had never visited the bar before, until the night of December 3, 2011. As sensitive Mel U. and I walked into the country-style tavern (decorated with deer heads) I immediately noticed the paranormal energy in the cabin. After looking around, appreciating its cool mountain-man décor, Mel and I sat down at the bar next to an elderly gentleman who seemed a bit tipsy. I once again felt something, almost as if it were right behind me.

I turned to Mel and said, "This place is totally haunted, dude."

She smiled.

Before she could respond, the man sitting next to us overheard me and said, "I've never seen you two here before."

"Yeah, this is my first time, and Mel's third time," I said.

"So you've never been here, you just walked in and you claim it's haunted?" he inquired.

"Yes!" I said with confidence.

"And you never heard of it being haunted?" he asked.

"No, I just know it, dude," I said.

The man immediately leaned over the counter and shouted across the bar to the owner, "Hey, Monty, is this place haunted?"

"Yeah, it is!" said Monty. "George is still here!"

The man at the bar looked back at me in drunken amazement.

"Wow, you were right!" he exclaimed.

Monty walked over to us and explained who George was, filling us in on all of the activity they have encountered. He said George's spirit is still very active, and that he and all staff members make a point to acknowledge George's existence.

George was the bar's previous owner from the 1970s to the early 1990s. Known for his great sense of humor, he died a little before his time due to Multiple Sclerosis in the early 1990s. Ever since, George's presence has been felt within the bar. Doors are said to open and close on their own, along with lights turning on and off on their own.

A bartender said that she had actually yelled at George a week ago after he kept turning off the lights. She had to turn them back on multiple times throughout the evening, and the only explanation was that George was up to his old tricks again.

The owner explained how he and a couple of customers witnessed a cup of beer fly off the counter when there was no one near it. This was unusual behavior because George's spirit is said to be very pleasant. Monty believes that George did it because he didn't like the woman whose drink it was.

Every night before closing up the bar, a staff member sets out three chairs in front of the front door for their visiting ghosts George, his sister Rose, and a past staff member named Pat. One night a staff member forgot to leave the chairs out. That night the bar was broken into.

What made our mouths drop was when a song came on and it seemed as though George started to join in using the K-2 Meter. The lights on the EMF detector were lighting up, increasing and decreasing to the beat of the song. It went on like this for almost two minutes. It looked very much like an Audio Spectrum Analyzer on a stereo.

"Wow, he's having fun," said Mel.

We were both amazed and baffled. We had never seen anything like it before. I very much regret not bringing my video camera into the bar. We could feel his energy becoming very strong, almost as if he were standing at the bar with us, rocking out to the music.

MONTY'S LOG CABIN
Year built: Circa 1970
5575 Highway 9
Felton, CA 95018
(831) 335-9969

### Roaring Camp Railroads

Nestled in the Felton redwoods on Graham Hill Road, Roaring Camp Railroads built in 1875 has a long history. Before Spanish explorers came to the vicinity in the 1700s, where Roaring Camp now stands on Bear Mountain, it was once

## The Santa Cruz Ghost Directory

inhabited by the Zayante Tribe. In the 1830s, a logger named Isaac Graham settled in the area and constructed Graham Hill Road for his logging company so that he could easily commute to Santa Cruz and back.

In 1875, the city began giving rides to passengers on the steam engines from the mountains to the beach. Roaring Camp Railroads got its name in 1963, when it was made into a tourist attraction. The pleasant Roaring Camp Railroads is now a preserved piece of history from the 1880s. The park has an old western appearance, making visitors feel as

*The Santa Cruz Ghost Directory*

if they have gone back in time when the trains first began to run.

Founder F. Norman Clark (1935- 1985) is said to haunt Roaring Camp after his death due to pneumonia at 50 years of age. According to local railroad historian, Ed Kelley, Norman's ghost still watches over the establishment. "Quite a few employees have experienced Norman peering through the shop door with a displeasing look on his face; others have simply heard his mumbling, but have never seen him," Kelley added.

Roaring Camp's Jane Doe, a 125-year-old, female skeleton was found on Bear Mountain located in Roaring Camp off of Graham Hill Road in 1996. Some workers were clearing the brush and saw their dog playing with a human bone, which led them to the corpse that still had remnants of clothing and items from the early 1870s. The skeleton was found wearing a leather vest, a loaded .32 pistol revolver, a knife, gold coins, a gold watch, glasses, and a bottle of liquor. Her death looked as if it had been caused by a .44 bullet shattering the lower-left portion of her rib cage. The bullet was lying underneath the skeleton when it was found. This courageous woman's spirit is said to still haunt Roaring Camp, after her murder over a century ago.

In recent years, hikers found human remains near the tracks at this historical landmark. The corpse was never identified and specialists couldn't predict whether it was a man or a woman because the pelvic region was missing. There have been no leads on how this person was killed. Whoever it was, though, is definitely trying to reach out and make their presence known. Ever since the body was found, trains keep stalling on their own during all hours of the night right where the corpse was found. Conductors claim to have repeatedly observed a woman crossing the tracks. As soon as they make the train come to a screeching halt, there is no one in sight. In 2009, a conductor claimed to see strange lights and shadows.

ROARING CAMP RAILROADS
Historical Landmark
Year established: 1875
5535 Graham Hill Road
Felton, CA 95018
(831) 335-4484
www.roaringcamp.com

## SANTA CRUZ

### Arana Gulch

Nestled in the heart of Santa Cruz is the stunning Arana Gulch. It has been known to be haunted for decades by the Ghost of Jack Sloan (Andrew Jackson Sloan), who was shot and killed by Jose Rodriquez and Faustino Lorenzana on the evening of February 11, 1865 along the old Arana Bridge (located on Soquel Avenue, next to Jeffery's).

According to local historian Phil Reader, the spirit of the 38-year-old has been seen on many occasions wearing a long, dark overcoat and a wide-brimmed hat, in or near the north end of the gulch. A member of the coroner's jury who investigated the killing said that this is what Sloan was wearing when he died. Sloan is known to appear on the anniversary of his death and has been reported by several eyewitnesses who spoke to S.C. Sentinel reporters regarding their encounters.

*The Santa Cruz Ghost Directory*

On July 25, 1895, 30 years after his death, a woman and her daughter were riding to town in their buggy when an apparition ran right out in front of them, and then vanished into thin air. Their description of the spirit and how it was dressed made the woman and her daughter believe that it was the ghost of Jack Sloan.

*Santa Cruz Evening News, July 26, 1895*

The second reported sighting was in 1913, by a large family who was living at the gulch at the time. The children came home to tell their mother about the new friend they had met in the gulch that day. They gave their Mother an exact description of Sloan. When he was 90 years old, one of these children verified the ghost story, also mentioning that his sister had seen Jack Sloan on several other occasions.

In 1932, the next sighting was reported. A family from out of town broke down on the side of the road when their car overheated. They claimed that a tall, thin stranger dressed in a dark overcoat came out from the bushes of the gulch and poured water in their radiator from the creek. To the driver's surprise, when he started cranking the automobile, he noticed that the stranger had faded back into the bushes.

In 1953, a group of five boys also encountered the spirit late one night. The Boy Scouts observed the apparition "gliding as it merged with the woods."

The last Jack Sloan sighting was recently, when a couple that lives along the gulch came forward with their story. They said they often saw Sloan crossing their deck at night in front of their sliding glass door, generally accompanied with a low-lying fog.

ARANA GULCH
Entrance at: Agnes Street
Santa Cruz, CA 95062

### The Asti

This aged bar located on Pacific Avenue in downtown Santa Cruz was built around 1920. The structure was once used as a speakeasy called the Crossroads until 1937, when it became the Asti Café. It is believed that several uncanny events happened on the property before 1937, creating paranormal activity.

Over the years, employees have experienced the unexplained at the Asti Café, particularly in the basement where it once looked as if splatters of blood stained the walls. The basement was once connected to all of the underground tunnels of downtown Santa Cruz, where several homeless people, criminals, and bootleggers are said to have lived or passed through. Former employee Brian Carey stated that the basement creeped him and other staff out so much, they literally just run in and out when they need to go down there. I spoke with a former employee who verified he would do it, too, and he's a big burly guy covered with tattoos.

"The ghost down there does not like me," the former employee stated.

A former janitor claimed to have heard disembodied voices near the bar and pool room where a light hanging from the ceiling has been seen unexplainably swinging.

Over the years owner Tara Gulielmo Muccilli had felt an unseen presence in the building, and never felt quite alone.

"I felt uncomfortable in the early mornings by myself," Tara explained. She said the feeling died down after the large windows were put in on the side of the building.

THE ASTI
Year built: Circa 1920
715 Pacific Avenue
Santa Cruz, CA 95060
(Downtown)
(831) 423-7337

### The Boardwalk Bowl

It is believed by some employees that the bowling alley is haunted by spirits who are said to make their presence known. Bowling pins are said to be knocked down on their own after hours, as well as manual toilets flushing on their own.

Around 2005 while the back patio was being renovated, human remains were found beneath the concrete. An employee shared with me that they were told the area was once an old graveyard from hundreds of years ago... but who knows.

BOARDWALK BOWL
Year built: Circa 1960s
115 Cliff Street
Santa Cruz, CA 95060
(831) 426-3324
www.boardwalkbowl.com

### Bocci's Cellar

The restaurant, bar, and bocci ball court was opened in 1925 by the Urbanis. The Italian immigrant family built the structure in 1885, and during their stay they lifted the house and built a large wine cellar. Bocci's Cellar's dining room and bar is located in this cellar, where astonishing paranormal activity is said to occur. Over the years, employees have seen ghosts, as well as witnessed objects moving on their own.

*The Santa Cruz Ghost Directory*

One employee has seen the ghost of an old woman in the restaurant on more than one occasion, sitting in the back corner admiring a picture. The first time the staff member had this encounter, the ghost-woman's back was turned so he was unable to see who it was. It was after hours, so the employee figured it was a manager or one of the owners. The staff member approached the ghost and when he tried putting his hand on her shoulder, his hand went right through her body. It was at this moment that he realized this entity was no longer living. The mysterious, long gray-haired ghost, clothed in a

Victorian dress, turned around and looked at him.

"She didn't have a face," he explained to me. The staff member saw her on a few other occasions always sitting in the same seat, admiring the Urbani Family photograph on the wall.

On a few occasions, the Urbani Family photograph was moved to another location in the cellar, and whenever it was, the paranormal activity would start up again. A bartender shared with me that she's been hit repeatedly by glasses that will literally just fly off shelves whenever the picture was moved. The phenomenon was obviously linked to this particular picture. When staff would put the aged photo back in its original spot, the ghostly activity would die down.

I was invited to investigate Bocci's Cellar after hours, so on October 13, 2012, at 2:13 am, local psychic medium Jena Reece and I began our investigation. Within minutes there was paranormal activity. The Mel Meter, which measures EMF, began to spike randomly in the middle of the Bocci Ballroom. We noticed the EMF increased as we walked toward the women's restroom. We stood in the middle of the restroom and asked the entity if they could please come closer to the device to make the numbers increase. Immediately, the meter started going up from 0.1 to 0.4 and then back down to 0.1 again.

Using the flashlight method (where the spirits turn the lights on and off) with two mini Maglites, (one for "yes" answers and one for "no" answers) we were able to communicate with at least three different spirits. One was an old woman who was waiting for her loved ones to come home from the war, another was male, and the third was the little girl on roller skates in the old Urbani family photo. The spirits confirmed that the little girl still roller skates throughout the restaurant, and that some others are still playing bocci ball at the venue.

BOCCI'S CELLAR
Year built: 1885
140 Encinal Street
Santa Cruz, CA 95060
(831) 427-1795
www.boccis.net

### Callahan's Pub

Callahan's, the biker-friendly bar, opened its doors in the early 80s. The building, located on Water Street, was previously used as a bar and lounge called the Fireside Lounge. Over the years, the owner, employees, and guests have all experienced unexplainable phenomenon and believe with certainty that the pub is inhabited by spirits of old patrons and friends.

Strong spiritual forces and energy are felt throughout the pub. Ghosts have been sighted, and objects moved on their own. A coffee maker turned on after it was unquestionably turned off minutes prior.

I spoke with bartender Lete Goodwin who has been working at the bar since 2001. She and several others feel the energy of their past friends, customers, and acquaintances on a normal basis.

"This isn't a normal bar. This isn't a place where people just pop in; this becomes a second home for a lot of people. Some have infinite connections to this place, so when they do pass, the pub becomes an emotional tie for them. I have lost some good friends who would come here frequently, and I know they still do. I definitely feel taken care of at the end of the night," Lete stated.

One night when Lete went into the walk-in refrigerator, a customer saw the ghost of a man follow her in. As she came out and was closing the door, she said the customer told her to wait for the guy that was still inside.

"Honey, we're the only people here," Lete said to the patron.

At that moment, the customer realized that he had just seen a ghost.

"He got so freaked out, he just said, 'I got to go!' and took off," she exclaimed.

A former bartender has seen male spirits within Callahan's sitting at the bar and just standing around. And, on one particular occasion, she was followed half way home by one of them.

*The Santa Cruz Ghost Directory*

CALLAHAN'S PUB
Year originated: Circa 1980
507 Water Street
Santa Cruz, CA 95060
(831) 427-3119

### The Catalyst

Once used as a little bowling alley until 1976, the Catalyst holds lots of history, memories, and energies.

Santa Cruz local John Manley and his wife both have had several encounters when working at the Cat from 2005 to 2010.

"I have heard, seen, and felt things that I could not ignore," he began. "There's a part in the main hall where both sides are lined with mirrors all the way down to the stage. Often after the club would close, and we'd be getting ready to walk out through the back door (because all the employees would leave through the back at night), you couldn't help but feel like you were being watched (through the mirrors) as you left," John shared with me.

"There was one night when my wife was working at the Rockers Pizza portion inside the Catalyst. It was about 2 o'clock in the morning and I was waiting for her to finish shutting down the pizza kitchen. I swear that I could hear music coming only from the main hall. It was like bluegrass music, and it was faint, but you could make out guitars playing. I immediately went and told my wife, - she is what we would consider a sort of medium, so she believed me, but she didn't stop doing her cleaning duties. I went back and sat on the counter and waited for her, but I didn't hear the music any longer. As I stared forward into the atrium, that's when I saw it. – A dark shadow of a thin man with long hair, who walked from the right to the left in my line of vision. How do I know it was a man? It's like when you're experiencing spiritual activity a part of you just turns into it. It's like sometimes you're around spirits and you know that they're bad because you feel uneasy; but in this instance I didn't feel that at all. Actually it felt like he was a guest who is just there to enjoy himself. But at the same time he felt like that was his place to be. Like he was always there. And then he was gone."

"It wasn't more than a week before I experienced something else, but it definitely wasn't that same energy. As I'm walking through the hall towards the back door I got this uneasy feeling like they (the ghosts) were rushing me. The whole time I'm walking through the center of the hall, I felt like they were staring at me from both sides through the mirrors on each side of me, so I started walking faster. I was like, 'okay, I'm leaving, don't trip.' But as I got closer to the door the energy increased, and by the time I reach the stage I could feel shivers up my spine; the energy just wasn't happy. As soon as I was outside, the door slammed behind me, and hard. In that very instance I obviously turned around to look at the door. In the window on the door I can see only what I can interpret as a white smoke-like radiance of some sort of face that I could not quite make out the details of. Even though it freaked me out, it didn't feel evil," John said.

THE CATALYST
Year established: 1976
1011 Pacific Avenue
Santa Cruz, CA 95060
(Downtown)
(831) 429-4135
www.catalystclub.com

*The Santa Cruz Ghost Directory*

## Cliff Crest Bed and Breakfast

The quarters were built in 1887 for the governor William Jeter and his wife, Jennie. The Jeters both lived in the house until they passed away.

The ghost of Jennie Jeter has been experienced by many guests and employees for decades at the Cliff Crest Bed and Breakfast. Several witnesses have heard the sounds of footsteps, and of furniture being moved in her room, along with finding pillows that had been rearranged and put in disarray.

*The Santa Cruz Ghost Directory*

*Jennie Jeter, 1890, public domain photo*

CLIFF CREST BED AND BREAKFAST
Year built: 1887
407 Cliff Street
Santa Cruz, CA 95060
(831) 427-2609
www.cliffcrestinn.com

## Coffeetopia

No one knows who truly haunts the building but some have theories. Within the last six months, the activity increased immensely after two customers named Steve and Nancy, who visited the shop daily, both passed away within a few months of each other. Steve was said to help set up in the mornings and pull out chairs. Amy, a staff member, said that since Steve's death chairs have been pulled out and moved on their own. Within the last few months she and Eli, another employee, have also witnessed "dishes flying off shelves" right before their very eyes. Recently, they heard the disembodied voice of former patron Nancy say, "Heelllooo."

Both Johanna and Amy have heard eerie sounds come from the attic and both agreed that one noise they both hear on occasion sounds like someone bouncing a ball on the floor.

They also feel as if they are being watched and followed around the shop on almost a daily basis. Johanna said that the radio has turned on all by itself and the volume is known to be turned up and down randomly.

Several years back, a former employee saw the ghost of an old woman in a Victorian dress inside Coffeetopia while unlocking the front doors one morning.

COFFEETOPIA
Year built: 1970s
3701 Portola Drive
Santa Cruz, CA 95062
(831) 477-1940
www.coffeetopia.com

## The Del Mar Theater

Former employees have heard unexplainable voices in the old dressing rooms, as well as seen dark shadow apparitions out of the corners of their eyes. The upper-level theater, where horror movies are usually played, also exudes abnormal energy at times, and where a lot of paranormal activity is said to occur.

An old employee named Barney is said to haunt the Del Mar since his fatal heart attack while on the job in the projection room. Some staff members believe that the former projectionist causes all of the paranormal occurrences within the building. During the days of 35 mm film, the projectors at the theater were known to jam, the lights in the projection room would flicker, and seats in the auditorium are said to have flipped down by an unseen force.

THE DEL MAR THEATRE
Historical Landmark
Year built: 1936
1124 Pacific Avenue
Santa Cruz, CA 95060
(831) 469-3220
www.thenick.com

## Dominican Hospital

The 17-acre facility was opened in 1967 by the Adrian Dominican Sisters, assisting mass amounts of people every year, providing several different types of services. There have been thousands of deaths and births that have taken place at this hospital on the east side of Santa Cruz on Soquel Drive. The Intensive Care Unit

(ICU) alone holds more than one thousand patients per year.

Not only is there residual energy that lingers from the births of babies, people passing, and even people who are in pain, there are ghosts who inhabit Dominican Hospital as well.

Over the years there have been stories of employees sighting ghosts of old nurses around the hospital.

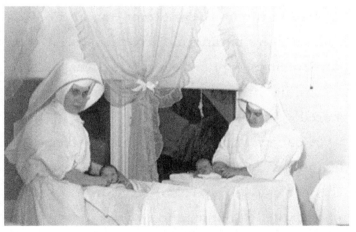

*Sisters at Dominican Hospital, Santa Cruz, photo by unknown*

Some employees talk about the mysterious "phantom baby cry" that's been allegedly heard by several Dominican engineers. Some claim to have heard the disembodied cries of a baby at random times around the hospital when there are no babies in the vicinity.

I spoke with an employee that I will call Jane. Jane has worked in the ICU for years and has seen and heard an abundance of spirits, mostly those who have just passed away in the prior Catholic Hospital.

"Within the first year of working in the ICU I began to have paranormal experiences. At first I didn't really accept or believe what was going on . . . until I had an experience of my own," she shared.

"A patient had died and it was one of the first deaths I witnessed at the hospital. I remember when he had just passed away, he was in the room to the left of me, and I was standing at the sink washing my hands. I thought to myself, 'Where is this person now?' Where is his spirit now?' And all of a sudden I felt something, like an energy just move through me. It walked through me from left to right . . . and it was him.

It was one of the first forms of verification that I got," Jane stated.

"At the hospital I've seen shadows in the hallway and in the utility room, which was once used as a trauma room. For a long time, I couldn't be in there with the door closed because it was just really creepy, but after a while I started being more open to it."

Every time local psychic Shelly Crowley visits the hospital, she sees a huge crowd of spirits standing behind the main building. Dressed in both hospital gowns and everyday attire, they seem to just be "waiting" for something.

DOMINICAN HOSPITAL
Year built: 1967
1555 Soquel Avenue
Santa Cruz, CA 95065
www.dominicanhospital.org

## Evergreen Cemetery

Established in 1850, the Evergreen Cemetery is the oldest graveyard in Santa Cruz County. It is one of the very first pioneer cemeteries in California and is known to have paranormal phenomena at all hours of the night, and even in broad daylight. For decades, there have been claims of paranormal activity at Evergreen; apparitions and multi-colored orbs have been observed by visitors, high EMF (electro-magnetic fields) have been detected as well as rapid temperature fluctuations.

The ghost of an elderly woman has been observed in the Evergreen Cemetery on many occasions. Some allege to have observed her sweeping the top of the stairs in the back of the cemetery. One transient said that he saw her clear as day in front of an old shack on top of the stairs, yelling obscenities and telling him to leave. When the traveler went back years later, he didn't see the old lady or the rustic shack. Apparently, there never was such a shack, others told him later.

*Possible spirit apparition, Evergreen Cemetery*

In 2012, after investigating Evergreen Cemetery, I was actually followed home by a spirit. She was by my side for weeks, until two psychics helped her cross-over and re-unite with her twin boys, which are also buried at the cemetery.

*For MUCH more information on my haunting, I suggest you check out my book, **ATTACHMENT: A Santa Cruz Ghost Story,** available on Amazon.com.

Additional Information:

- Years back, a woman claimed to have been grabbed by an unseen force through the bars of the crypt. She said the spirit would not let go.

EVERGREEN CEMETERY
Historical Landmark
Year established: 1850
Evergreen Street
Santa Cruz, CA 95067

## The Golden Gate Villa

Nestled on Beach Hill, the extravagant Golden Gate Villa was built in 1891 for Major Frank McLaughlin and his new family. McLaughlin married a woman with a three-year-old daughter named Agnes, and soon after, he adopted her as his own. As time went on, his daughter grew into a beautiful young lady, who was known to rarely date and still lived at home with her father at 34 years of age. After a while, rumors spread through the town that Frank had romantic feelings for Agnes.

*The Santa Cruz Ghost Directory*

*Agnes McLaughlin (center with guitar), circa 1900s, courtesy of the Golden Gate Villa*

*Santa Cruz Sentinel, November 17, 1907*

*The Santa Cruz Ghost Directory*

*Major Frank McLaughlin, circa 1900, public domain photo*

On the second anniversary of Agnes's mother's death, McLaughlin had a horrific arrangement that he regretted soon after. On November 16, 1907, Agnes came home one day and loosened her corsets to lie down in bed. Major Frank McLaughlin entered her room, and without any hesitation, shot Agnes in the temple with a .44 caliber handgun. McLaughlin then took a fatal dose of cyanide, taking his own life, along with his adopted daughter's.

It is claimed that the Major's motive was clearly because of his guilty passion for Agnes. It is confirmed that in McLaughlin's last letter he wrote, "I love her so, and so I take her with me."

After Agnes's death, a large, jeweled, stained-glass window was made in her honor. A few strands of her hair were also placed in the glass. Legend has it that Agnes still haunts the old Victorian quarters. "Accounts of a lavender-dressed spirit floating about the mansion persist ..." Santa Cruz Sentinel, 1975.

The present owner stated that "Agnes's ghost still wanders the house," and a former owner feels like she's being watched, especially while she's cleaning the home, according to a Metro Santa Cruz article on October 29, 2003. Sometimes if you're lucky you'll catch a glimpse of Agnes's spirit standing at her old bedroom window, or drifting throughout the mansion.

THE GOLDEN GATE VILLA
Historical Landmark
Year built: 1891
924 3rd Street
Santa Cruz, CA 95060
\*\* PRIVATE RESIDENCE – NO TRESPASSING.

### Holy Cross Cemetery

In 1885, six wagons carrying human remains were moved from Holy Cross Church on the Westside of Santa Cruz to the old Holy Cross Cemetery. The remains consisted of mostly Ohlone Indians, and some Spanish soldiers, Yankee loggers, and European immigrants. Half of them were children under the age of 12. The 2,436 bodies were all buried together in one unmarked mass grave in a corner of the north side of the cemetery, and still reside there today.

In 2012, while visiting the old, eerie cemetery, I spoke with a spirit from the large, unmarked burial plot. After asking them several questions and received answers with my ghost hunting equipment and my intuition, I had learned that many of the spirits were unable to rest due to the way their corpses were mistreated and not reburied properly.

Recently, in November of 2016, the county finally decided to show some respect to the dead, and gave them a memorial plaque, with all their names listed, as well as planting seven redwood trees around the memorial. I pray that some of the restless spirits will now find peace.

*Old Holy Cross Cemetery*

A few hundred yards away at 2271 7th Avenue, sits the most recent addition to the cemetery, where the deceased have also been moved from one section to another. Some believe that the moving of remains can disturb the dead and lead to paranormal activity, such as hauntings.

The cemetery's most well-known phantom that passes through the old careworn grave yard, is the ghost of Jack Sloan (See Arana Gulch story). Since the 1950s, Sloan has been seen by multiple witnesses floating through the cemetery.

Other spirits have been sighted in and in front of both the Holy Cross cemeteries, particularly at night.

Spirits of the cemetery are known to venture out and around, and sometimes make a visit to Rossi's Body Shop and Towing Company across the street from the old Holy Cross Cemetery, and in front of the additional graveyard. Over the years, employees have had unnerving and unexplainable paranormal experiences, and consider that the activity is due to the fact that the shop lies between two cemeteries.

Years ago, one employee heard what sounded like footsteps in the gravel past the door while he was working on a car late one night. Thinking it was an intruder, he got up suddenly but didn't see anyone.

Another employee heard a disembodied voice coming from the side of the building one night and upon inspection didn't find anyone there.

One tow truck driver claims that for years he has seen a dark shadow figure on the property periodically. Sometimes he'll see them walking through the yard, or standing near the front gate. Even with a bright porch light on, they'll allegedly show themselves on occasion.

"Sometimes when I'm backing into the shop and I look into my rearview mirror, I'll see a shadow figure standing there near the gate."

(OLD) HOLY CROSS CEMETERY
Year established: 1873
Capitola Road Extension
Santa Cruz, CA 95062

## Highway 17

Highway 17 is known to be one of the most dangerous roads in California. The twenty-six-mile, winding route makes its way through the mountains from Scotts Valley to Los Gatos, California. For generations, many drivers and passengers have reported seeing apparitions walking and/or standing along the highway, and some have even seen them sitting in the back seats of cars. Others have alleged seeing white vaporous clouds floating over the lanes.

Some have claimed to see the ghost of a 17- or 18-year-old girl walking along the road at twilight.

Along with seeing spirits wandering the area, visitors driving through sharp turns have heard sounds of collisions and tires screeching to a halt, and upon inspection, there are no reckless drivers at the scene.

The apparition of an Ohlone Indian man has been seen for centuries walking on the side of the highway. Legend has it he causes all the accidents on 17.

HIGHWAY 17
Year established: 1930s
(The freeway that runs through Santa Cruz and Santa Clara)

## Jeffery's Restaurant

A ghost of an old waitress has been seen on occasion by at least two employees. She was said to have worked at the restaurant long before it was renamed Jeffery's, until the time of her death. Her full-body apparition has said to be seen around the diner, usually standing in front of a table with a pen and paper in hand. She has also been sighted walking through the swinging doors near the bathrooms.

According to local psychic Shelly Crowley, Jeffery's has a bunch of phantom customers, mostly seniors. "The place is packed," Shelly stated. "It's like trying to find a place to sit!"

JEFFERY'S RESTAURANT
Year built: 1979
2050 Soquel Avenue
Santa Cruz, CA 95060
(831) 425-1485

**The Jury Room**

The old dive bar located on Ocean Street, across from the court house definitely has its share of hauntings. One of the ghosts who makes his presence known frequently is said to be the spirit of a former owner who occasionally still sits in the same place that he did while he was alive at the end of the bar. Former employee Brian Carey and other bartenders have not only seen the foggy apparition from the corner of their eyes, but straight on as well.

Over the years, the atmosphere began to feel more eerie, and the hauntings increased, becoming more intense, especially after the early 1970s when the demented, local serial killer and necrophiliac, Edmund Kemper, visited the bar regularly. It is claimed Kemper would sometimes bring his deceased victims with him and keep them in the trunk of his car while he chatted with local police officers over beers. No one had any idea Kemper was capable of such ghastly behavior, putting behind them the fact that he murdered his grandparents when he was 15 years old. He secretly hoped that some of the officers he spoke with at the bar would figure him out, and when after his 10th nauseating murder they still hadn't, he turned himself in.

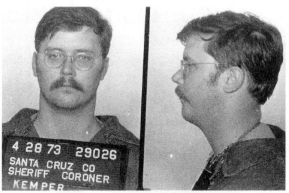

*Mug shot of notorious serial killer, Edmund Kemper, Santa Cruz, CA, public domain photo*

A couple of his victims, the young, innocent female hitchhikers from around the county, are believed to haunt the Jury Room property. Sensations of sadness are felt at times, as well as the strong presence of one or more young female spirits.

The bar is also believed to be haunted by old patrons, whose ashes have been scattered on the roof of the Jury Room. Glasses are said to move on the bar, and doors open and slam close on their own, even when they are locked. Unexplainable drafts within the building cause objects to move on their own, too, such as an American flag, and dollar bills tacked to the ceiling.

Individual voices and disembodied conversations have been heard, and unseen entities felt. Spirit orbs have also been sighted in the bar after hours by several former employees.

In 2013, I was offered to investigate the Jury Room, but I never did. Honestly I was scared to after a couple psychics warned me about investigating there. They both felt something dark and almost evil lingering at the bar. One told me to not go alone, and make sure I have someone spiritually powerful with me, due to a dark entity they sensed in the back.

THE JURY ROOM
Year built: Circa early 1960s
712 Ocean Street
Santa Cruz, CA 95062
(831) 426-7120

*The Santa Cruz Ghost Directory*

**Mark Abbott Memorial Lighthouse**

On February 28, 1965 a local 18-year-old surfer by the name of Mark Abbott tragically went out to catch his last wave. In memorial of his death, his parents Mr. and Mrs. Chuck Abbott donated a new lighthouse at Lighthouse Point, to the city that same year. Mark's ashes are said to be laid in an alcove at the lighthouse.

Local legend has it that the cute, quaint, brick nautical museum overlooking the Santa Cruz Bay is haunted by Mark Abbott's ghost.

"I never feel his presence, but you know he's here," said Jesse Shank, a surf museum worker. Santa Cruz Sentinel, 2001.

MARK ABBOTT MEMORIAL LIGHTHOUSE (AKA
SANTA CRUZ SURFING MUSEUM)
(Santa Cruz Lighthouse)
Year built: 1967
701 W Cliff Drive
Santa Cruz, CA 95060

**Mission Santa Cruz**

Built in 1791, the Santa Cruz Mission holds the legend of Father Andrés Quintana. The Father was known to beat and whip the Ohlone Indians while they were working at the mission, some as young as eight years of age. He was also said to sexually assault various women, and so his cruelty got old fast. One dark, stormy night on October 12, 1812, Father Quintana was ambushed by several members of the tribe. They could no longer bear his malicious acts. Some of the Indians choked Quintana to death, while others crushed his testicles with rocks from the mission's foundation. He was then neatly tucked into his bed as if he had died in his sleep.

*Mission Santa Cruz*

Many believe Quintana's spirit still curses and roams the area, known as "Haunted Hill," trying to inflict pain and poverty on anyone he can.

Witnesses claim his ghost has been seen dressed in a brown robe and sandals standing at the altar inside the mission, and is even seen walking through the park across the street.

According to several Santa Cruz Sentinel articles I found, Andrés Quintana as well as some Indians are buried underneath the haunted Holy Cross Church located next to the Mission.

*The eerie Holy Cross Church on Mission Hill*

*Replica of Mission Santa Cruz*

In 2012, local Sensitive Mel U. and I visited the Mission during the witching hour one night. We received responses on the Ghost Radar while using dowsing rods. We also recorded an EVP of some type of tribal drumming.

On the 200-year anniversary of Padre Quintana's death, local reporter Mat Weir, psychic Jena Reece, and I visited the haunted mission. Standing near the property, we believe to have spoken with both Indian spirits and with Quintana himself. Quintana's presence was strong; we sensed that he didn't want us there.

When I asked if he'd like us to leave, the flashlight turned on. Not leaving quickly enough, an unseen force poked local psychic medium Jena Reece on her side, causing her much discomfort.

*Mission Santa Cruz*

While we were walking along the side of the Santa Cruz Mission, Jena saw the ghost of a middle-aged woman in a white gown walk across School Street and disappear before reaching the other side of the road.

MISSION SANTA CRUZ
Historical Landmark
State Historic Park
Year built: 1791
144 School Street
Santa Cruz, CA 95060
(831) 425-5849

## The Mystery Spot

The Mystery Spot was discovered in 1939, and was opened to the public in 1940 for touring. This particular location is definitely bizarre. It is known as a gravitational anomaly, where the law of physics does not apply. Some think it's all an optical illusion. Others consider there is a vortex at the Mystery Spot creating the abnormal surroundings and generating a supernatural portal to another dimension. Many employees, locals, and researchers believe that long ago an alien spacecraft crashed into the mountains in the vicinity of the Mystery Spot, causing all of the weird anomalies at the park.

## The Santa Cruz Ghost Directory

"Most of us here believe there's a large alien spaceship underground and the motor is still going in circles, and that causes the large gravitational pull that makes us lean." This is quoted from a Mystery Theater film, investigating the Mystery Spot on Dailymotion.com. It is said that the ghosts of the aliens who died in the crash haunt the vicinity of the Mystery Spot.

Many of the Eucalyptus trees located around the attraction are twisted into corkscrew shapes. Normally Eucalyptus trees grow straight with small bends here and there. A theory that some scientists have is that the trees are trying to counteract the pull of the Mystery Spot.

As well as other phenomena, the majority of cameras have a hard time focusing in the cabin to take pictures and to record videos. Camera's batteries are known to drain quickly when inside the slanted house, too.

A Mystery Spot staff member stated that there was an elderly man who used to come to the attraction once or twice a week because it made him feel younger. The visitor claimed that he would take in the energy waves that are created by the Mystery Spot, and that this energy gave him "oomph." Several others notice that their migraines go away when they reach the cabin.

*The Mystery Spot*

Over the years, people have claimed that the attraction is haunted, and that ghosts are drawn to the gravitational pull. Some have claimed to see bright, colorful, glowing orbs around the Mystery Spot at night.

THE MYSTERY SPOT
Year originated: 1940
465 Mystery Spot Road
Santa Cruz, CA 95065
(831) 423-8897
www.mysteryspot.com

**Paradise Park**

Long ago, Paradise Park Masonic Club was used as a gunpowder facility known as Powder Works, from 1864 until 1914. One tragedy that will never be forgotten was the accidental explosion that occurred on April 26, 1898. Locals saw sparks in the air and felt a huge blast from two miles away. "Most of the men killed in the blast had been torn apart, their bodies tossed dozens of yards in all directions," -Santa Cruz Sentinel. On that occasion it had killed eleven workers, and over the years, several other explosions had occurred on the land, killing both residents and employees.

## Explosions at the Powder Works Startled This City.

### ELEVEN EMPLOYEES MEET DREADFUL FATE.

*Santa Cruz Sentinel, April 27, 1898*

The vicinity on and around Paradise Park is claimed to be haunted by past Powder Works employees. Level-headed workers would see ghosts near the location where the former employees died. It is said that the ghosts of the former workers are known to make their appearance on the eve of the explosions at the front old Powder Works covered bridge.

Years later, the site was restored into a private community with a view of the river. In 1997, a couple that had lived there complained about their home being haunted. They alleged that on many occasions they were able to hear voices around the house – voices that spoke a foreign language.

*The Santa Cruz Ghost Directory*

PARADISE PARK
Year originated: 1924
211 Paradise Park
Santa Cruz, CA 95060
(831) 423-1530
**PRIVATE RESIDENCES –NO TRESPASSING.

## Pogonip

According to local lore, "The Ghost of Pogonip" has been haunting the vicinity ever since an Ohlone Indian was sentenced to death by his tribe for standing up to his elders. With his dying breath, he cursed the tribe and swore to haunt them for eternity. Many believe his curse on the tribe and on the area is the cause of strange deaths and peculiar events in and around Pogonip.

Several locals and visitors said that they saw spirits throughout Pogonip, along with hearing chanting.

Surrounded by hiking trails, high on a hill in Pogonip Park stands the condemned Pogonip Clubhouse, which is also claimed to be haunted. Built in 1911, the house was used as the Santa Cruz Golf and Country Club until 1930. In 1935, it was reopened as the Pogonip Polo Club, until WWII, when it was used as a rehabilitation center for the soldiers at war. In 1948, the Pogonip Club was back in action hosting sporting events until 1986 when it became condemned.

According to a Santa Cruz Sentinel article from 1988, "Guard Shawn MacDonald, who patrols the property, including the club grounds, recounted how he was doing his nighttime check on the building one recent night, and without warning or human interference, the lights went on. Another guard refused to go inside again after, during a solitary patrol he heard footsteps following him one night."

*The Pogonip Clubhouse*

In 1987, the clubhouse was used as "Grandpa's house" in the motion picture: *The Lost Boys, (1987)*. Since then, it has been is known by numerous locals as "The Lost Boys House".

POGONIP
333 Golf Club Road
Santa Cruz, CA 95060
(831) 420-5270

## Pono Hawaiian Grill

My friend Timmy, owner of the fabulous Hawaiian lounge in downtown Santa Cruz, hit me up in 2013 to investigate his restaurant; after he and former workers had a few unexplainable occurrences. Timmy first showed me some eerie video footage his security cameras had caught just a week before. Several stacks of glasses that were on a counter and against a wall literally flew forward, as if an unseen presence had hit the stack of glasses from the center. It was clear and obvious on the footage that the stacks of glasses which are always there, didn't just fall over. Two bartenders were standing in the vicinity when the glasses shot out which completely spooked them both.

A Pono waitress shared with me that she always sensed there was a spirit there, but it never scared her. She just could feel that there was someone around.

Cooks have claimed to hear a child crying near the bar in the early hours of the morning, as well as feeling a presence within the structure.

I brought two psychics there on separate occasions and they both believe a little girl haunts the establishment, and had been killed in or in front of the building. One psychic said it could have been a possible car crash.

PONO HAWAIIAN GRILL
Year built: Circa 1920
120 Union Street
Santa Cruz, CA 95060
(831) 426-PONO
www.ponohawaiiangrill.com

## Railroad Tracks

Ghost trains have been heard and witnessed around the county over the years, particularly along the beginning of Highway 9 in Santa Cruz, where trains no longer go.

"Five of my friends and I were walking late at night along the railroad tracks. We had been walking back to campus from The Garden of Eden when we saw an extremely bright light behind us on the tracks. It made a sound like a train, so we all got off of the tracks and waited for it to go by. The light came closer and closer, but it never passed us. The light just went out, and its sounds evaporated," a local student shared.

Some runners had a similar experience in the same area with a ghost train, though they actually witnessed a train filled with passengers with blank faces pass by them. They didn't think much of it, since the train seemed real and the passengers much alive. A few minutes down the trail, they came across a man who was cutting up a giant tree that had fallen on the tracks.

They then wondered how the train could even pass the tree. Getting spooked they decided to turn around and found that both the woodsman and the tree had mysteriously vanished.

RAILROAD TRACKS
(Along the very beginning of Highway 9)
Santa Cruz, CA 95060

## The Red Room

The historic Victorian on Cedar Street was built in the late 1800s and was once used as a brothel, before being used as the Santa Cruz Hotel. Legend has it that a forlorn prostitute took her life by hanging herself in the building upstairs, where the women's restroom is presently located. Her ghost, as well as others, are said to haunt the elegant eatery and bar.

Employees and guests have experienced very unusual encounters over the years, particularly when they are alone. Objects are said to move on their own, disembodied footsteps and voices have been heard, and apparitions have been seen.

"I heard footsteps as if someone had entered the bathroom. The footsteps got louder and it almost seemed as if someone was pacing back and forth in front of my stall. I looked under the door and realized there was no one else in the restroom other than myself."

I spoke with a couple employees who both believe the building is haunted and have each had an encounter.

"That's so weird," a waitress said to me when I asked about the haunting. "We were just talking about that."

The young employee had only been working at the restaurant for a little over a month but was well aware of its ghost stories.

A young bartender who I will call Marie, stated that she sees two spirits in her peripheral vision around the lounge area, usually around 4 am, when she's alone in the structure a few times a week.

Marie shared with me that a woman who looked to be in her late twenties wearing a long pale yellow Victorian dress has been sighted near both ends of the bar and in the kitchen.

"She's the one that appears the most . . . she's just kind of there observing everything," Marie said.

A young man in a brown three-piece suit and a top hat is the other spirit that's sighted most frequently, walking around the establishment and standing near the entrance of the lounge.

"I'm comfortable with them here. It's not negative; they're not being a menace, they're just here, like we're all existing together," Marie explained.

They do, on the other hand, like to get into a little bit of mischief at times.

"We'll get a lot of weird calls, especially right after I see the ghost with the three-piece suit. I answer and they'll hang up, or I'll answer and there's no one there at all; and that happens at least two to three times a week," concluded Marie.

The phantoms also like to move items, such as keys that have to constantly be replaced. "I'll hang up the keys, turn my back, look back, and they'll be gone," Marie declared with frustrated amusement.

THE RED ROOM
Bar, restaurant, and lounge
Year built: late 1800s
200 Locust Street
Santa Cruz, CA 95060
(831) 425-1913
www.redrestaurantandbar.com

## Sake – Japanese Steak House and Sushi

During the turn of the century, the land where Sake now sits was once occupied by the Italian American Hotel. While it was used as an inn, legend has it that the mafia was known to hang out in the dwelling. Local historians also claim a murder took place on the property.

In the 1960s, Adolph's Restaurant was built in place of the hotel. This is when the ghost stories began to arise. There were reports of paranormal activity near the buffet, the kitchen and in the restrooms. Past employees alleged feeling and hearing the unnerving presence, as well as noticing objects move on their own, such as plates that were mysteriously being stacked in the kitchen, and some falling on the floor and breaking. Some individuals actually claimed to see the spirit and described him as a tall, dark male dressed in 40s attire with a long coat and hat.

I went to Adolph's in 1998 with a friend, without knowing any of its background or haunted past. As soon as we entered the building, I sensed it was occupied by a spirit. The air was oppressive, the atmosphere unearthly. My friend's mom happened to work there at the time, so I figured I should at least ask if anyone else felt an entity in the building.

"Is this place haunted?" I asked my friend.

"Yes! How did you know?" she asked.

"I can just tell," I said.

The unexplained activity went on and became more intense over time. It was then that the owners decided to get professional help to try and rid the place of the unsettling presence, so they contacted the Berkley Psychic Institute. It is not known if a psychic did indeed visit the restaurant, but the hauntings are claimed to continue to this day.

Adolph's closed a few years later, and the China 1 Buffet took over for a short period of time, as did Fuji Restaurant; before being sold to the present owners, who transformed the building into a Japanese steak house.

Fuji staff claimed never to have spoken with former Adolph employees about the hauntings, but report seeing the same dark shadow man at times within the structure.

SAKE- JAPANESE STEAKHOUSE AND SUSHI
Year built: 1960's
525 Water Street
Santa Cruz, CA 95062
(831) 427-0182
www.sakejapanesesteakhousesushi.com

**The San Lorenzo River**

According to legend, the town's first Caucasian visitor was a shipwrecked sailor who wasn't accepted by the Indians. The tribe saw him as an intruder and sentenced the sailor to death. One of the tribe members warned the sailor of his tribe's intentions, and when his clan found out, they condemned him to death as well. With the Indian traitor's last breath, he vowed to haunt his people forever. The "Spirit of the San Lorenzo River" is said to have terrorized the Indian tribe until he divested them all.

Many feel this curse lives on, as well as some of the Ohlone Indians forever haunting certain areas of the river.

THE SAN LORENZO RIVER
Off Highway 9
Santa Cruz Mountains, CA

## Santa Cruz Beaches

According to local lore, the ghost of a woman known as, "The Lady of the Sea" is said to haunt several beaches in Santa Cruz. It is claimed that long ago she had drowned in a possible shipwreck, and her spirit still endlessly wanders. She has been sighted normally at dusk, or sometimes at night, and when the moon is full. "The Lady is described as very pale and typically garbed in black flowing clothing. Upon nearing spectators, she usually vanishes, sometimes with a cackle," Santa Cruz Wiki. Legend has it, she was involved with some of the night surfers near drownings; possibly helping to prevent the surfers from losing their lives in the sea, just as she had.

SANTA CRUZ BEACHES
Santa Cruz, CA 95060

*The Santa Cruz Ghost Directory*

**Santa Cruz Beach Boardwalk**

For over a hundred years the Santa Cruz Beach Boardwalk has been a place for both the living and the dead to enjoy. Ghosts have been seen walking on the boardwalk even in broad daylight. Two psychics I spoke with both had similar encounters while visiting the historic amusement park. They would pass by a few people and think nothing of it, until they would turn around only to see that there was one less person there.

*Santa Cruz Beach Boardwalk, Photo by Birdo Photo*

There are also private tunnels running beneath the boardwalk, which some employees claim to be haunted. On a few different occasions workers have witnessed the ghost of a boy around thirteen years of age running through the dark underground halls, only to disappear seconds later.

At least four untimely deaths have occurred on the historic roller coaster The Giant Dipper since it was built in 1924. All four of the victims stood up during the ride and flew out of the train and died.

*The Giant Dipper, Santa Cruz Beach Boardwalk, circa 1920s, photo by unknown*

*The Santa Cruz Ghost Directory*

The first death occurred on September 21, 1924, when sixteen-year-old Walter Fernald Bryne flew forward in front of the train and was crushed to death.

## WALTER FERNALD BYRNE, ONE OF BEST LIKED AND PROMISING LOCAL YOUTHS, KILLED IN ACCIDENT AT BEACH DIPPER

*Santa Cruz Evening News, September 22, 1924*

The second fatal accident happened on March 30, 1943 when nineteen-year-old James Piner stood up and fell onto the roof of the tunnel, where he then rolled off onto a catwalk, fracturing his skull, as well as having severe lacerations on several parts of his body. He died at the Santa Cruz Hospital two days later.

The third tragedy took place on July 6, 1958 when 22-year-old Peter Alfred Abila died at the scene after wiggling out from the safety bar and falling 65 feet to the ground.

*The Santa Cruz Ghost Directory*

The fourth reported death I found happened on July 13, 1972 when thirteen-year-old Edward Crooks fell from the top tracks to lower tracks and was hit head on by the train and died instantly.

# Roller Coaster Fall Kills Boy, 13

*Santa Cruz Sentinel, July 13, 1972*

Walter is said to haunt the roller coaster and has been observed a number of times by former employees and riders. The ghost is usually witnessed at night after closing on the back of the train by ride operators. Tourists have reported sitting next to a boy dressed in older clothing on the Dipper, and he vanishes sometime throughout the attraction. Along with

*The Santa Cruz Ghost Directory*

sighting a full-body apparition throughout the years, ride operators have claimed to feel a tug on their sleeves, or a tap on their shoulder when no one is in the area.

Pizza One near the bumper cars has had some unexplainable activity particularly around 2012, when multiple staff members had the same eerie encounter with whom they call, "The Barefoot Ghost". While closing up for the night, employees would notice bare foot prints randomly appear across the floor at times after mopping.

Neptune's Kingdom (now a miniature golf course and arcade) was once used as a heated, indoor salt water swimming pool known as the Plunge from 1907 to 1963. At least five deaths took place within the structure. They were all men, and four were teenagers.

The first death took place in 1935, when a 67-year-old man named T. Tallaert died of a heart attack while swimming. He was found floating face down in the pool.

In 1937, the second death at the plunge occurred. The victim was 16-year-old Richard

Albert Carona from Watsonville, and his cause of drowning was said to be unknown.

In 1958, 14-year-old Raymond Johnson had died to negligence, after he was caught in an underwater drain.

One year later in 1959, two more deaths occurred together. 15-year-old James Hagan, and 16-year-old Kenneth K. Matsumoto of Castroville, drowned after nearing the deep end without swimming ability.

*Postcard of the Plunge, Santa Cruz Beach Boardwalk, circa 1930s*

*The Santa Cruz Ghost Directory*

# YOUTH DROWNS IN CROWDED BEACH PLUNGE

*Santa Cruz Evening News, April, 1937*

The old structure is said to be haunted by its drowning victims and leaves an eerie vibe, particularly on the second floor on the wall of history.

A past employee shared with me that he had unexplainable encounters on occasion, such as seeing a frightening translucent face in the video monitor in the miniature golf course.

Others have claimed to see dark, sinister shadows form and move throughout the haunted course.

*The Santa Cruz Ghost Directory*

*Neptune's Kingdom, Santa Cruz Beach Boardwalk*

Another former employee claimed to have uncanny encounters while working in the restaurant inside Neptune's Kingdom. Not only did he feel watched when he was alone, he witnessed cooking utensils move and fly off hooks and shelves.

The Boardwalk Arcade (Casino) has been standing since 1907, and in recent years, staff members have seen a ghost of a tall man in the laser-tag room. One worker told me that she refuses to close the laser-tag department due to having too many creepy sightings and experiences.

*The Boardwalk Arcade, Santa Cruz Beach Boardwalk*

A former employee who worked at the old time photo shop inside the Casino said that she would occasionally capture ghostly apparitions in the photographs.

The Cocoanut Grove is another haunted spot at the amusement park. Most reports have been about poltergeist activity that goes on at the Grove after hours, although a ghost of a little girl with blonde hair and a pink dress has been seen on occasion running through the ballroom and dining room during the day.

*The Cocoanut Grove, Santa Cruz Beach Boardwalk*

Employees have claimed that chairs move around and get stacked on their own and security guards hear strange, disembodied sounds such as a harmonica playing late in the night.

Some employees and locals claim the Cocoanut Grove is haunted by the ghost of a man named "Woody."

SANTA CRUZ BEACH BOARDWALK
Historical Landmark
Year built: 1907
400 Beach Street
Santa Cruz, CA 95060
(831) 423-5590
www.beachboardwalk.com

### Santa Cruz Memorial

Malicious paranormal activity is believed to occur at night in the old, colossal Santa Cruz Memorial Cemetery, built in 1862. Housing a mortuary and mausoleums with halls full of graves, it is said that some of the deceased roam the 25-acre property.

The most common legends consist of seeing faces on tombstones, shadows stirring overhead, and hearing unearthly voices in the dark. Orbs can be seen by the naked eye, along with full body apparitions.

Several ghosts that have been spotted tend to be wearing Victorian-style clothing or they look homeless. (There was a homeless camp next to the cemetery for years where many destitute people perished.)

*Santa Cruz Memorial*

A ghost that has been seen most frequently is dressed in overalls and holds a shovel. Some locals say he was once a groundskeeper for the cemetery.

Some attest that spirits from the graveyard tag along and hitch rides with visitors back to their residences. Two locals claimed to have had the same experience several years ago. Ghosts followed them home from the cemetery and both of their houses were haunted for months afterward.

In 2015, while driving past Santa Cruz Memorial with local psychic Shelly Crowley, she noticed a group of spirits near the fence.

"I see three women dressed in Victorian clothing," she stated. "They are standing right at the fence and waving to us... Do you know them, Aubrey?"

"Possibly," I said. "I do communicate with spirits there, and have visited Catherine Logan's (wife of first owner of Brookdale Lodge) several times; so maybe it her."

Shelly smiled and nodded.

SANTA CRUZ MEMORIAL
Year established: 1862
1927 Ocean Street Extension
Santa Cruz, CA 95060
(831) 426-1601
www.scmemorial.com

## Santa Cruz Mountain Tunnels

The tunnels in the Santa Cruz Mountains are known hot spots for ghost hunters. In 1879, a tragic incident occurred at the Laurel and Wright tunnels under Highway 17, killing 32 workers. A gas explosion blew some of the miners to bits making it impossible to recover the remains of each victim. Many of the workers' remains are still there today, more than 100 years later, now buried beneath the soil.

*"Would the scenes within the tunnel and about the entrance be faithfully pictured, it would send a thrill of horror through every reader of the Sentinel. The stench of burning flesh, combined with the escaping gas, is almost overpowering anywhere near the portal. The cabins are filled with mutilated Chinamen, some shrieking with the excruciating pain they are undergoing; others praying in their native tongue to their countrymen to kill them and put an end to their suffering, or beseeching the God of Fire to have mercy upon them and cease his torments. In most of the cabins, tapers are burning, the perfume from*

*which serves somewhat to temper the sickening odor of roasted flesh,"* Santa Cruz Sentinel, November 22, 1879.

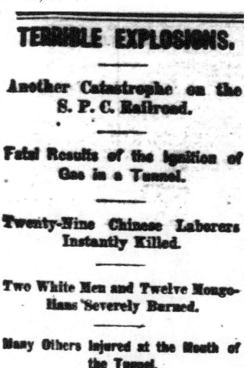

*San Francisco Chronicle, November 19, 1879*

"Yet in January 1880, the company brought a new crew of Chinese workers to finish the cursed tunnel. They burned incense and etched prayers upon the support timbers prayers to drive away the devils. Yet the curse proved too powerful. The terrified men refused to enter the tunnel, let alone finish the project." –Ryan Masters, "Horrors of the Summit Tunnel," hiltromper.com

Another disastrous incident occurred only a year later in May of 1880. A train travelling at high speed flew off the tracks near the Wright Tunnel. More than half of the 125 passengers were thrown from the railroad, killing 15 and severely injuring 50.

*Illustration of the 1880's train wreck in the Santa Cruz Mountains, public domain photo*

## The Santa Cruz Ghost Directory

According to author and paranormal investigator Jeff Dwyer, many ghost hunters have observed orbs, light anomalies, apparitions, and EVPs from the tunnels' entrances. Sounds of screaming, crying, and moaning have been recorded by various ghost seekers. Other paranormal enthusiasts have captured amazing EVPs of what sounds like the "ghost train" near the Laurel Bridge, where no active trains currently travel.

SANTA CRUZ MOUNTAIN TUNNELS
Year built: 1879
Santa Cruz Mountains, CA

## Santa Cruz Museum of Art and History

Established in 1996, the Museum of Art and History was once the site of the old county jail until the early 1980's. Residual energy lingers there from former inmates, as well as some of the historical artifacts that are within the museum. It is also claimed to be haunted by ghosts, according to a Sentinel Cruz Sentinel article from 1998. Museum director Chuck Hilger shared some of the hauntings that take place at the Santa Cruz Museum. "Every once in a while, we get some strange noises and some strange sounds, which we don't know where they come from or why they occur; and they do occur," he shared. He also pointed out that a certain large, heavy door has been seen and heard opening and closing on its own. Some of the unexplainable activity that occurs there, such as electrical shortages is blamed by workers from it being spirits from when it was once a jail. –The jail where notorious serial killers, Edmund Kemper and Herbert Mullin stayed, their cells adjacent to each other.

Receptionist Kirsten Kvam is also a believer in the museum being haunted. "It's something about the building. When you're on the third floor, it always sounds like there are doors opening and closing and there's nobody there," Santa Cruz Sentinel, October 12, 1998.

Kathleen Moodie, a museum curator shared how they were planning on honoring the spirits of the museum for the upcoming Day of the Dead event in 1998. "There have to be spirits because we have all these artifacts that probably belonged to people and are infused with their auras," she shared with the Sentinel.

This particular museum holds an abundant amount of energy, I think. Being so sensitive to energies, it can be almost overwhelming for me in there at times; to the point where my knees get weak, I break into a sweat, and I have trouble breathing. Any sensitive, or empath will know what I'm talking about. This place has history.

SANTA CRUZ MUSEUM OF ART AND HISTORY
Year built: 1890
705 Front Street
Santa Cruz, CA 95060
(831) 429-1964
https://santacruzmah.org/

### The Sunshine Villa

The Sunshine Villa, previously the old McCray Hotel, holds plenty of history within its walls and surroundings. Before the classic Victorian was built on the property in the 1860s, and became a hotel in 1879, the Ohlone Indians performed sacred rituals there and utilized it as burial grounds. For almost a century, the property was incessantly bought and sold, and was abandoned for almost a decade. Police reports state that while the Sunshine Villa was condemned, it was occupied by drug dealers, homeless people, and cultists. The cultists are said to have held satanic rituals throughout the building.

Notorious serial killer Herbert Mullin resided there as well back in the late 1970s, during the peak of his killing spree. Mullin was known to practice satanic rites in the tower above.

It was in the 1960s when the old McCray Hotel re-opened that claims of ghost sightings began to arise. Former employees claim to have been touched by an unseen force while working within this aged structure. Another local claimed that while living at the hotel he would see a blue mist materialize in room number 2. Windows and doors are said to open and close on their own, in addition to unexplainable sounds and footsteps. Housekeepers and other staff members have reported, "Cold presences, mysterious blue lights and the voice of women calling from the shadows," according to a Metro Santa Cruz article in 1999.

A friend of mine once worked at the Sunshine Villa and encountered a couple unexplainable events, such as a light turning on and off on its own when the room was unoccupied, as well as being touched.

"One time I was walking the food cart down to the dementia floor and I felt like something was gently pushing my lower back for a couple seconds.

I heard a story about a woman in the dementia ward who had never really spoken before, just moaned, but one night she woke up and yelled a man's name, the name of the resident who used to live in that room who had passed away there."

A local psychic feels that the spirit of a woman is trapped in the Sunshine Villa; she was murdered there long ago. The sensitive believes that the woman's death was covered up somehow and she is still waiting for someone to help her uncover her murder.

Accounts of bloodshed, rituals and dire karma, on an ancient Indian burial ground appear to create a space for ghosts to occupy. Today the Sunshine Villa still remains on Beach Hill, presently as a retirement home for the living ... and the dead.

Additional Information:
-     The creepy old McCray Hotel was the inspiration of Alfred Hitchcock's movie, *Psycho*, 1960. (For more information on Alfred Hitchcock and his former haunted estate, see the "Hitchcock Estate" story.

SUNSHINE VILLA
Historical Landmark
Year built: 1860's
80 Front Street
Santa Cruz, CA 95060
\*\* PRIVATE RESIDENCES – NO TRESPASSING.


**Surf Bistro and Bakery**

Built in 1949, the bistro is said to be haunted by a Canadian Freight train hopper who was once a regular at the location. His ghost has been claimed to be witnessed within the establishment at times by both guests and the current owners. Other paranormal activity includes hearing a disembodied male voice at times, and witnessing objects such as cooking utensils and pictures move on their own.

SURF BISTRO AND BAKERY
Year built: 1949
415 Seabright Avenue
Santa Cruz, CA 95062
(831) 600-7787

## Red, White, and Blue Beach

Red, White and Blue Beach is known for its ghostly goings. It is documented that when the beach was open to the public, dozens of campers, locals, and tourists had unexplainable encounters there and nearby. One of the oldest legends that has been told by locals for generations is about "the window that doesn't exist." While walking the beach late at night, many guests say they have seen a window lit up on the hill overlooking the water. Witnesses have described the window as cathedral-like. Some claim to have even seen movement and full body apparitions pacing in front of the ghostly window. As the sun rises, there is no house to be seen – just an empty hill.

On the cliffs, overlooking Red, White, and Blue Beach, stands a cottage known as "The Edwards' House." It is said the home was built and owned by a sea captain in 1857, who is believed to be the spirit haunting the vicinity today. As soon as the Edwards family moved into their new home in 1965, they noticed a black rain slicker and hat hanging by the back door that didn't belong to any of them. They later started to see the ghost of a sea captain wearing that exact outfit. This ghost is known to roam the perimeter of Red, White, and Blue Beach and has been seen by hundreds of people. The Edwards would also see the ghost walking out their back door.

The Edwards' daughters were constantly awakened by something that would viciously shake their beds at night. Their brother didn't believe them, so he traded beds with one of his sisters. The next morning the Edwards' son reported feeling like the bed was shaking and moving so violently he first thought it was an earthquake.

The next horrifying disturbance was when a large, heavy navy picture hanging on the Edwards' wall, was ripped off by an unseen force. The framed photo flew five feet and crashed down into the hardwood floor, embedding glass slivers into the wood. Another uncanny experience occurred in 1975, when owner Kathy Edwards was almost hit by a large potted plant. It flew approximately twelve feet toward her in midair. Luckily, her daughter caught it before it caused Kathy any bodily harm.

One skeptical visitor was laughing about the place being haunted, and within seconds, a drawer near him opened and a baby shoe flew out and hit him on his forehead. Kathy Edwards saw the visitor become a believer after that. Many visitors took the story seriously, including psychic Silvia Browne (RIP) from Campbell, California. She and other psychics envisioned victims being killed and buried on the property. One psychic said he saw a girl named Gwendolyn being murdered there around the turn of the century. Kathy confirmed that this event did in fact occur when she and her husband Ralph dug up a skeleton while putting in a barbeque pit one day. The human remains were examined by an expert, who said the skeleton was from a young woman, buried approximately 70 to 80 years ago.

Doors slamming and footsteps heard throughout the home is nothing compared to what the Edwards family has dealt with. Kathy's perfume bottles were known to clatter around a lot, and many heard sounds of shattering crystal coming from the vicinity as well. Countless amounts of the Edwards' household items were known to disappear and reappear in different locations. Some have even witnessed objects flying through the air. Lights turn on and off after the Edwards are in bed and many campers on the campground complain about the flickering lights that are seen throughout the night on endless occasions.

Additional Information:
- Witnesses have seen moving blobs and bolts of light, and some have also captured the anomalies on film.
- Many have reported observing the ghost of the old Sea Captain strolling around the camp grounds as if he were flesh and blood, and then suddenly disappears.
- It is said that a woman was murdered on the beach by her boyfriend, and that her ghost haunts the vicinity as well.

RED, WHITE, AND BLUE BEACH
5021 Coast Road
Santa Cruz, CA 95060
redwhiteandbluebeach.com

(It has been noted that the beach closed after the owner and manager, Ralph Edwards passed in 2014. RIP.)

## University of California, Santa Cruz (UCSC)

The Henry Cowell Ranch, now the UCSC campus, was owned by the Cowell Family back in 1850. Only six months after Henry's death, Henry and Alice Cowell's second to youngest child of five, died tragically on the ranch, and her spirit is said to have haunted the town for over a century.

On May 14, 1903, 40-year-old Sarah Agnes Cowell took a trip down to the old Cowell Ranch, where she liked to pick wildflowers. Sarah and the housekeeper were riding a high-spirited horse and buggy across the fields together one day when disaster struck. One of the wheels from the buggy hit a rock, scaring the horse, making it bolt. Tragically, Sarah Agnes flew from the buggy and broke her neck, killing her instantly.

# A FATAL ACCIDENT

## MISS SARAH COWELL KILLED NEAR HER FATHER'S KILNS.

*Santa Cruz Sentinel, May 15, 1903*

Sarah's spirit still haunts the Ranch and has been witnessed on many occasions in 'The Haunted Meadow,' also located on the UCSC campus. The first detailed sighting of Sarah's spirit was reported to the Sentinel in 1975. One night in 1971, a group of students were wandering the meadow, when her ghost frightened one of them beyond belief. The student ran back down the trail and met up with the group alleging to have heard distinct footsteps behind him when there was no one in sight.

*The remains of Sarah Cowell's buggy that she road to her death, Santa Cruz, CA*

In 1973, Sarah was spotted in the upper quarry on the UCSC Campus. A student claimed to see her transparent, cloaked spirit casting an eerie shadow beneath the quarry. The local legend of Sarah Cowell's spirit has been told from generation to generation, likely keeping her spirit alive.

Another ghost by the name of Lily appears in 'The Haunted Meadow.' Legend has it that the beautiful young transient woman lived in the field in the 70s and died there. Lily's apparition has been seen a countless number of times walking around the vicinity in either rags, or completely naked.

On the third floor of Building B at Porter College, occupants have complained over the years of suddenly awakening in the night, feeling as if someone was strangling them. The bottom floor of Building B has been condemned supposedly because of reoccurring paranormal incidents. There have been several reports made of objects flying across rooms, random noises, such as voices heard incessantly, along with malicious feelings and energies. The ground floor is known to some students as "The Bermuda Triangle."

The last notorious haunting on the University's Campus also took place in Porter College, but in Building A. Years ago, a student hung himself on the fifth floor. It is alleged that he has been occasionally seen walking down the halls of the building. Multiple eye witnesses claim to have seen him in dark pants and a white shirt.

"The road up to the University past the entrance is haunted by the ghost of some type of old timer. He looks like a working man from I'd say about a hundred or so years ago, way before they built the campus. I have seen him and so have others I've spoken to. He appears briefly at the side of the road at random times it seems," A UCSC student claimed.

Additional Information:

- Sarah Agnes Cowell has been seen in the shadows of the trees, mostly in the afternoon or before twilight. She is known to be wearing a long, pale yellow dress and a bonnet.

UNIVERSITY OF CALIFORNIA, SANTA CRUZ (UCSC)
Year established: 1965
1156 High Street

*The Santa Cruz Ghost Directory*

Santa Cruz, CA 95060
(831) 459-4003
www.ucsc.edu

**The Walnut Avenue Incubus**

*Incubus: A male demon, or spirit who prays on sleeping women to engage in sexual intercourse.*

According to a Metroactive article in 1999, a "sex ghost" is said to have once haunted a residence on Walnut Avenue in downtown Santa Cruz, California. Allegedly, before he died, the rapist lived in the home and would take advantage of the servant girls who resided there as well. A woman who lived in the house around the 1920s confirmed at least one of the rapes in the front room.

Unaware of the house's uncanny past, five women moved into the home around 1993, and had to figure out for themselves who else occupies the house. In addition the unpleasant residual energy that lingered, three of the women began to have very disturbing and unbelievable experiences in the old dwelling, experiences they would never forget.

One of the victims, Olivia, kept having reoccurring sex dreams and claimed to wake up tired, as if she had just experienced a long night of intercourse. Cynthia, another woman who lived in the home, was able to see the young entity, and claimed that over time it became more volatile. Their housemate, Anna, had also been haunted by the incubus.

"Now this was a very tough girl. But the minute I asked her, she turned and looked at me and burst into tears. She told me that she'd been having these experiences that when she went to sleep, it felt as if somebody were stroking her hair and touching her body."

"We burned some incense in the house and that got rid of him for a while. But then sometime after that, Catherine (another housemate) and I were sitting in kitchen, and no one else was home and we heard this voice say, 'I want you.' It was crystal clear, but at the same time almost like a fading echo. I mean, the hair on our arms stood straight up, and Catherine said, 'Do you think he's back?' We checked inside the house and outside, but nobody else was around," Metroactive article, 1999.

Three days later, Olivia had another dream, ". . . there were all these people out in the backyard dressed in turn-of-the-century farm clothes, knocking on my bedroom window. In my dream I sat up in bed and looked out the window, and they told me, 'You have to wake up because Michael is back.'"

The dilemma became extremely overwhelming and upsetting, especially after two of the women witnessed some dishes in the dish rack being rearranged on their own. They received advice and insight from a psychic who sensed that the rapist once lived in the home with his previous victims. This is when Olivia got into contact with the woman who previously resided there during the 1920s, who knew about a reported raping.

After figuring out who the unpleasant entity was and why he was there, Olivia claimed to speak to him for two weeks, addressing that they are not servants, and that he needs to respect them or leave. She said that the activity completely stopped after her confrontation and they believe that the vicious entity finally went somewhere else.

WALNUT AVENUE
Santa Cruz, CA 95060

### The Water Street Bridge

In May of 1877, two men by the names of Francisco Arias and Jose Chamales were hung from the Water Street Bridge for being suspected of murder. It was known to be the last lynching of mixed heritage brought on by a mob of locals. Before these men took the leap to meet their maker, they were given a final shot of whiskey and said their last words.

*The Santa Cruz Ghost Directory*

Since the execution, people have claimed to see ghostly apparitions of the men near the bridge, sometimes hanging.

*Hanging at the Water Street Bridge, 1877, Santa Cruz, California*

*The Santa Cruz Ghost Directory*

WATER STREET BRIDGE
Year built: 1870's
Water Street at River Street
Santa Cruz, CA 95060

**The West Cliff Inn**

Built in 1877 by Sedgewick Lynch, West Cliff Inn was known as the Lynch Mansion until 1909, when it was used as a sanitarium run by a well-known local woman by the name of Mary Jane Hanly. Miss Hanly had a reputation for having "mystical powers" and treated her patients using holistic remedies. She was said to have once revived a man after he had drowned in the ocean nearby. For years she was known as "The Mother of the Boardwalk" because of her love and compassion in helping others, as well as taking in people who were completely broke.

In 1923, Mary Jane Hanly opened the 'Hanly Hospital' on the left side of the Hanly Sanitarium, where surgical procedures were performed without any type of anesthetics or sedation. At times, murder victims were treated at the hospital, dying soon after being brought in.

In 1937, Miss Hanly became very ill and was bed ridden in the hospital where she died on August 31, 1937.

After Hanly's death, the building was donated to the Sister's Hospital, then used as a poor house, then an office, and eventually dilapidated. In 2004, the structure was transformed into The West Cliff Inn, and ghost stories began to arise. Local legends say a "lady in white" has been seen looking out the top window of the 3rd story. No one knows for certain whom the woman could be, but after investigating the West Cliff Inn, I believe it is the ghost of Mary Jane Hanly; who chooses to stay at the property and just may for all eternity.

WEST CLIFF INN
Historical Landmark
Year built: 1877
174 West Cliff Drive
Santa Cruz, CA 95060
(800) 979-0910
www.westcliffinn.com

*The Santa Cruz Ghost Directory*

## White Lady's

The Legend of the "White Lady" of Santa Cruz has been told for more than a century, and her ghost has been seen by an abundance of eye witnesses. The White Lady is also notorious for haunting the surrounding areas, such as down Ocean Street Extension, and on occasion she has been observed at the Santa Cruz Memorial Cemetery at the end of the road.

According to legend, it all started back in 1870 when a German fellow sent away for a mail-order bride from Massachusetts. Shortly after his young, beautiful bride arrived, they got married and settled down in the stone cottage, now known as "White Lady's." Legend has it that the "old lush" got drunk nightly and forced his bride to wear her wedding dress, and then he would beat her ruthlessly. When the bride decided to leave her husband, he found out about her plan and made sure she didn't follow through with it. He beat her to death, decapitated her, left her body in the house, and set their home ablaze.

*The Santa Cruz Ghost Directory*

*The White Lady's house in 1959 before it burned down (again). Several locals claimed to see her ghost looking out the top window. Photo courtesy of the Graham Hill Water Treatment Plant*

Soon after the bride's disappearance, "hordes of people," as stated in a Santa Cruz Sentinel article, began reporting seeing a glowing ghost wearing a wedding gown floating around the area. She was also seen looking out the top window of the abandoned house before the fire. In the 1970s, White Lady's became a huge drinking and make-out spot for teenagers. Various locals claim to have seen The White Lady in her blood-soaked wedding dress with her head tucked underneath her arm.

"Her gown is bloody and her hair is wool-looking, and she has been heard mumbling, 'Get out of here before I kill you.' My father told me the story as a young boy and I of course did not believe it, until I saw her myself." ¬J. Crowder, Strange USA

One dark night in April 2011, I went by the deserted lot to take photos. I was standing in the middle of the road on Ocean Street Extension facing the property. It was so dark I couldn't even see my hand in front of my face. It was dead silent except for the crickets that seemed to chirp in sequence. All of a sudden, the temperature dropped and I could hear footsteps walking toward me on the gravel. The footsteps sounded as if they were only a foot or so away when they stopped. I spun around and took off running to the car.

I returned to the vicinity near White Lady's months later with local sensitive Mel U. and our friend, Sara. When we first arrived, we sat in the car and I read aloud the legend of the White Lady from my first book, Supernatural Santa Cruz, to get into the mood and to let Sara in on the story behind it.

We began asking if anyone was there that would like to speak with us. Mel and I both felt a strong female presence come toward us. We sat the flashlight down and within a minute or so it turned on and off by itself. We asked the White Lady to turn it off for us and she did each time we asked.

I misplaced my recorder, but after finding it, we noticed that the Ghost Radar picked up the word "Record," and the flashlight had turned on at the same time.

The following are some questions we asked using the flashlight when the White Lady's answers were Yes.

Mel: Were you murdered?

Mel: Did your husband murder you? If your husband murdered you, can you turn the light on?

Just to verify, Mel repeated the question.

Mel: Is that a yes? If your husband murdered you, can you turn the light on really bright?

The light got brighter a moment later.

Mel: If your husband used to beat you, can you turn the light on?

Mel started to feel a cold spot near her.

Sara: Maybe you need a new flashlight. Maybe something is wrong with this flashlight.

Mel and I laughed.

Me: All right. We have a skeptic here. Can you please turn on the light and make it flash on and off for us?

It did as I asked.

Mel: Can you do that again for us, please?

It flashed twice more.

Mel: Can you turn the light on really bright if your husband killed you in your wedding dress?

The light got extremely bright and wouldn't turn off.

After asking the White Lady to turn off the flashlight, we began asking more questions.

Mel: Did your husband beat you to death?

Right then the Ghost Radar picked up the word, "Entirely," and the flashlight came on immediately afterward.

We heard noises around us in the woods and asked the White Lady to verify that it was just animals. The light came on.

Me: Are you stuck on this property?

Me: Do you want us to help you? Do you need help?

The Ghost Radar picked up the word, "Writing."

Mel: Did you used to be a writer?

Me: Maybe she's referring to the story I wrote in my book about her.

The flashlight turned on, literally, a second later.

Me: Are you happy I wrote about it, making you famous?

The light came on bright for three seconds and then turned off.

Mel got out her pendulum and started using it to contact the ghost. You can use one to communicate with spirits by letting them move the weight and swing it horizontally or vertically.

"Does your name start with the letter B?" Mel asked.

The pendulum started swaying vertically for, "No."

"Does your name start with the letter C?"

It then started swaying horizontally for, "Yes."

Just then a car drove by, their stereo blasting Nekromantix, a Psychobilly band Mel and I both love. As I enthusiastically pointed it out, the spirit tugged on the pendulum while Mel was holding it. (It can actually be seen on the video footage; I captured it being pulled down by an unseen force and then springing back up.)

*The Santa Cruz Ghost Directory*

"Wow!" Mel exclaimed. "She just tugged on my pendulum!"

"Do you not like that music?" I asked. "Can you turn the flashlight on if you didn't like that music?"

The flashlight quickly turned on.

"We like it. Sorry."

"So, your name begins with the letter C?" Mel asked.

The pendulum started swaying horizontally once again.

"Can you turn on the flashlight if your name starts with a C?" I asked.

The flashlight turned on immediately.

It was getting late and soon it would be time to go.

"Would you like us to come visit you again sometime?" I asked.

The flashlight turned on and shined very brightly for about six seconds and then slowly turned off.

*The Santa Cruz Ghost Directory*

*The author at White Lady's, 1999*

WHITE LADY'S
Ocean Street Extension at Quail Crossing Road
Santa Cruz, CA 95060
** NOTE: A NEW HOUSE WAS BUILT ON THE PROPERTY IN 2012, AND IS NOW A PRIVATE RESIDENCE, SO NO TRESPASSING.

**Wilder Ranch**

Before the historic ranch was used as a dairy farm, the land was known as Rancho Arroyo del Matadero, and later on named Rancho del

Refugio. The property was occupied and used by Ohlone Indians as slaughtering grounds for cattle until 1854, when a man by the name of Moses Meder bought the land and created a dairy farm.

In 1871, The Wilder family took over the ranch and created a new and updated creamery. For almost a century, the Wilder Family resided on the land and maintained the business until 1969. In 1974, it was taken over by the California State Parks.

Several of the aged houses and ranch-style buildings from the mid to late 1800s still stand on the property today, keeping the old-time spirit alive. I spoke to a docent at the ranch and asked if she had ever heard of any ghost stories or sightings that had taken place there.

"We do have a resident, but he's only seen on certain days," the elderly woman, dressed in Victorian attire, replied. She also senses energies around the ranch, particularly inside the Wilder's former house.

The cow barn built in 1850 is also haunted, and an apparition of a middle aged man has been witnessed standing in the stalls.

In 2013, using some of my ghost hunting equipment (pendulum, Ghost Radar and flashlight); as well as my senses, I spoke to a spirit in the cow barn who claimed to have died at the historic Ranch. He confirmed that he was a Wilder, and that he had passed away on the property after an accident in his 30's. His energy was sweet and relaxed and he seemed content with still being at his family's old estate.

I spoke to a Wilder Ranch historian and told her about my encounter and conversation with the ghost in the barn.

"That sounds just like the Wilder's grandson, Billy Wilder, who died here after a hunting accident," she shared with me.

The historian then brought me over to the Wilder's Family Tree in the park's office and showed me who she was referring to. There, it stated, "Williamson (Billy) Wilder -1926 to 1963" (36 years of age) (-Note: he told me he had died in his 30's, as well as being a Wilder, and dying there.)

"That's got to be him!" the historian said to me with confidence.

Returning home after my investigation I looked for articles on Williamson "Billy" Wilder's death. On January 6, 1963, he accidentally shot himself in the chest with his 20-gauge automatic shotgun while climbing through a barbwire fence at Wilder Ranch.

WILDER RANCH
Historic State Park
Year established: 1871
1401 Coast Road
Santa Cruz, CA 95060
(831) 423-9703

# SCOTTS VALLEY

### Alfred Hitchcock's Late Estate

It was in 1940 when Alfred Hitchcock and his family bought the beautiful Spanish-style adobe, which was built in 1926. The Hitchcocks used the 200-acre estate in the Santa Cruz Mountains as their second home until 1972.

According to famous psychic Sylvia Browne (RIP) the fabulous old Hitchcock estate is said to be haunted and stained with residual energy from Santa Cruz's dark past. Browne visited the estate back in the 90's, when some friends of hers were interested in buying the large estate. Before Browne even entered the property, paranormal activity began. The psychic saw the ghosts of two large beautiful dogs lying on the ground guarding the gate at the front entrance. When she got closer she noticed the dogs were very ill and foaming at the mouth, as if they had been poisoned. When Browne arrived at the former Hitchcock estate, she told the hostess, Lavona about her encounter. Lavona seemed surprised and asked Sylvia how she knew about the dogs. Browne reminded her that she's psychic.

As Sylvia entered the five bedroom home, she immediately was horrified.

"All I could see were walls covered in bloody handprints, and cowled figures standing everywhere, watching us, like cloaked and hooded monks with nothing but darkness where their faces should have been." -Sylvia Browne, *Visits From the Afterlife*

While touring the estate, Browne also saw ghosts of both a man and a woman.

"... some movement outside the barred window caught my eye. I looked to see a small, thin, gray-haired woman in a black dress with white cuffs, a white collar, and a white apron. A very dapper man in a black suit was standing beside her."

Weeks later Browne saw an old photograph of the Hitchcock family. Standing in the photo with them was the older gentleman and woman that she saw in the yard.

She was so overwhelmed by visiting the home and seeing such frightening images.

"... I'm convinced that the land the house is built on is holding imprints of centuries of Godless evil, darkness that could take centuries more to be neutralized ... The bloody handprints on the walls of the Hitchcock house are the only traces these sadistic pseudo-Druids' victims left behind ... Whoever is living here now, I would love to hear from you. But whether I do or not, please know that you're in my prayers." –Sylvia Browne, *Visits From the Afterlife*

*Alfred Hitchcock's Former Estate, Scotts Valley*

More on Alfred Hitchcock:

The legendary, local writer, filmmaker, and producer Alfred Hitchcock was known for his thriller and horror movies, particularly his hit flick, *Psycho*, made in 1960. The Sunshine Villa located on Front Street (see Sunshine Villa story)

## The Santa Cruz Ghost Directory

is what inspired Hitchcock to write the film. The home was the Old McCray Hotel at the time. The place not only looked haunted, it was. The decrepit structure was so eerie and enchanting, that Hitchcock made the Bates mansion in his movie Psycho very similar to the haunted hotel, located on Beach Hill in Santa Cruz.

That same year, Hitchcock won an Academy Award for best director, and also received an honorary doctorate for "magnificent accomplishment in the world of cinema," presented by The University of California, Santa Cruz.

In 1961, a strange event took place in Capitola that inspired Hitchcock to write his next famous film, The Birds, released in 1963. Late in the night on August 21, 1961, huge flocks of seagulls "invaded" the area from Pleasure Point to Rio Del Mar Beach. Hundreds of seabirds fell from the sky and collided into homes. Scientists could not determine why the birds came down is such an odd fashion.

*The Santa Cruz Ghost Directory*

*Alfred Hitchcock at his former estate, Scotts Valley*

Hitchcock was a local resident of Santa Cruz County until 1974. The creative genius, also known as "the Master of Suspense," was said to be very serious, but also very funny at times. One of Hitchcock's most famous quotes was, "The length of a film should be directly related to the endurance of the human bladder."

After directing more than fifty films, the eighty-year-old legend died peacefully in his sleep from kidney failure on April 29, 1980, in Bel Air, California. Hitchcock was then cremated, his ashes spread along the Pacific

*The Santa Cruz Ghost Directory*

Ocean. His funeral was held in Beverly Hills at the Good Sheppard Catholic Church. Although Hitchcock is no longer with us, his time in Santa Cruz County still echoes with his glory.

*Alfred Hitchcock, public domain photo*

ALFRED HITCHCOCK'S LATE ESTATE
(Now known as: Heart O' the Mountain)
Year built: 1926
705 Canham Road
Scotts Valley, CA 95066
(831) 406-1881
www.heartothemountain.com
** PRIVATE WINERY– NOT OPEN TO PUBLIC.

## Bruno's BBQ

Part of an old 1920s structure still stands, nestled in a corner within the Kings Village Shopping Center in Scotts Valley, and currently occupied by Bruno's BBQ. Before Bruno's moved to its present location in 2003, the building was used by several different venues, and became partially remolded, except for one part of the building which is believed by various patrons and a bartender to be haunted. An old, classy bar still remains, as well as the second floor banquet room, with a cocktail lounge, where the paranormal activity occurs.

*The upstairs cocktail lounge, Bruno's BBQ*

## The Santa Cruz Ghost Directory

A former bartender at Bruno's BBQ told me that for many years guests have gotten the feeling that the upstairs was inhabited by a ghost or two. Some have claimed to have seen or heard things that they couldn't explain. I asked if the venue was haunted after I felt an unseen presence watching me from the top of the staircase that leads to the banquet room. The bartender said that other people have also told her that they get the feeling of being watched. "Go upstairs and tell us what you feel," a waitress said to me. Of course I took up her offer and headed up the staircase where the energy seemed to change drastically with each step. It wasn't an un-easy energy whatsoever, but it was obvious that something or someone still hangs out in the structure.

When I reached the top of the stairs, I got a strong sense of a man in the cocktail lounge near an old original fireplace. At that moment, my Ghost Radar said, "Engineer." I began taking photos and while I was focusing my camera on the bar in the cocktail lounge, I noticed two orbs that were both the size of a baseball shoot past me. The energy then got even more intense for that moment. It caught me by surprise since I had just arrived, and I've only experienced something similar on a few other occasions. Unfortunately, my camera was still focusing and didn't capture the orbs in time; but I will never forget it.

It's a mystery who haunts the restaurant, but there are theories. The Bartender that I spoke with said that she thinks it could be haunted by the man who built the original, remaining part of the building. I got the sense that she was right about that.

BRUNO'S BBQ
The Kings Village Shopping Center
230 Mt Hermon Road
Scotts Valley, CA 95066
(831) 438-2227
www.brunosbbq.com/

*The Santa Cruz Ghost Directory*

### Cinelux

The theater's second auditorium is inhabited by a spirit that has made guests, as well as employees, feel as if they are being watched.

Former manager Chet Bauerle said that he felt the presence I had heard about, and that he doesn't like to be alone in the second auditorium without another worker present. After a midnight showing of *Paranormal Activity 3*, Chet stated that some guests came out of the theater and said, "We don't know what was more scary, the theater or the movie!"

Another eerie incident took place in 2009. One of Chet's coworkers went in to clean

Auditorium 2, when he came upon an elderly woman in the theater who was very upset. Apparently, this lady was yelling at him, so he went to find a manager. Within less than a minute, Chet and this staff member came back to the auditorium where the woman had just been, but she was gone. "There is no way she could have gotten out of the auditorium that fast. We checked the back doors; we checked everything, and no sign of the lady."

"Upstairs in the projection booth, I'd go as fast as possible to start movies, thread them up, do whatever I had to do and get out of there. It felt hostility up there, like something didn't want me in there. I was never actually touched, but it was almost like something was pushing you out. As soon as you open the door to the projection booth, you were not welcome."

The third ghost is believed to be the spirit of a former owner, who has been seen walking up the staircase by an employee, and was also sighted in the office by several construction workers. A newer employee told Chet that the spirit of a man kept following him around. After describing his features, Chet concluded that he was being trailed by the old owner.

Some of the theater's staff members claim to feel his presence watching over them, and even looking over their shoulder.

CINELUX
226 Mt. Hermon Road
Scotts Valley, CA 95066
(831) 438-3260

# SOQUEL

### Blue Ball Park

As the legend goes, the hill located at Anna Jean Cummings Park (known as Blue Ball Park) is said to be haunted by a young couple who overdosed and died there in the 1970s. Several people have claimed to see the ghostly couple standing on the hill dressed in hippie attire at night. Others claim to have seen their silhouettes sitting beneath a tree holding hands at sunset.

ANNA JEAN CUMMINGS PARK
(AKA BLUE BALL PARK)
461 Old San Jose Road
Soquel, CA 95073

### The Daubenbiss House

Some probably wonder what the story is behind the big, old Victorian on the hill overlooking the Soquel Village, so I'm here to tell you ... The Georgian style home was built in 1867 and bought by California pioneer, John Daubenbiss who built and ran a sawmill, and the first flour mill in California. He and his wife Sarah moved into the home shortly after it was built and resided there until their deaths.

*The Daubenbiss House, circa 1880*

The couple had 11 children, and 5 of them unfortunately didn't survive adulthood. The Daubenbiss' suffered the loss of their first child, 14-year-old John F. Daunbenbiss in 1862; -his cause of death is unknown. They lost an infant in 1869, and Joseph Daubenbiss (18 years), in 1873. That same year, they lost another son, 17-year-old James B. Daubenbiss who tragically drowned in the bay. I have yet to uncover who their 5th child was, that left this earth much too soon.

The Daubenbiss house was used for parties, receptions, and even funerals. It was much lived and died in. John's wife Sarah passed away in their house in 1891, at 62 years of age. Five years later, John Daubenbiss struck ill and also died in the home on February 10, 1896, at the age of 79. He was buried next to his wife and children at their family plot in the Soquel Cemetery down the road, which he had founded years before.

The house was then sold and bought, and sold, and bought again; and during that time, ghost stories began to arise. A former owner stated that she personally never saw a ghost there, but she definitely could feel a presence. That presence is believed to be the ghost of John Daubenbiss, who has been seen standing on the front upper balcony of his beloved home, still overlooking the town that he holds so dear.

*John Daubenbiss, circa 1870*

*The Santa Cruz Ghost Directory*

Additional Information:

- Spirit orbs have been sighted around the outside of the Daubenbiss House.
- Disembodied voices and unexplainable sounds have been heard.

DAUBENBISS HOUSE
Year built: 1867
4500 Soquel Drive
Soquel, CA 95073
\*\*PRIVATE PROPERTY- NO TRESPASSING.

### The Soquel Cemetery

The Old Soquel Cemetery, also known as the Eternal Home Cemetery, is located in the rolling hills within the city of Soquel, California. For many years there have been stories of the graveyard being haunted.

High EMF has been discovered in broad daylight, orbs have been captured on film; and ghostly shadows have been witnessed.

*The Santa Cruz Ghost Directory*

SOQUEL CEMETERY (ETERNAL HOME CEMETERY)
Year established: 1852
550 Old San Jose Road
Soquel, CA 95073

## WATSONVILLE

### Hecker Pass

The ghost of a young woman in a red dress has been seen walking along Hecker Pass (Highway 152) for generations by several witnesses. She is known to hitch rides from taxi drivers. They pick her up and then claim that she vanishes suddenly. One cab driver from Watsonville had an experience with the ghost in the red dress, not knowing she was a spirit until the following day. It began one night at around midnight. The taxi driver was near Mount Madonna when a beautiful young woman waved him down and asked for a ride. Contemplating on whether or not to give the lady a ride, (since it was late) he decided to take the woman to her destination. The ghost asked to stop near the bottom of Mount Madonna next to a house that stood alone. He felt the young woman get nervous when they approached her home. The spirit suddenly jumped out of the car and bolted toward the house, not paying her fare for the cab ride.

The next day, the cab driver went to the residence he had seen the young woman run into the night before. An elderly woman opened the door and he began telling her what had transpired the previous evening, describing the young woman in the red dress. The homeowner picked up a framed photo of her two daughters and showed it to the taxi driver. Immediately, the driver recognized the young lady and pointed her out. Shocked, the mother then replied that her daughter had died in a car accident years before as she was heading home. She offered to pay the cab driver, but he insisted that she keep the money.

HECKER PASS
(About a mile up Hecker Pass)
Watsonville, CA 95076

**Mount Madonna County Park**

Sarah Miller's spirit has been seen around Mount Madonna since her death in 1879. The land was owned by her father, Henry Miller "The Cattle King," one of Gilroy's founders who had bought the land only months before his daughter died. One hot summer day in June, eight-year-old Sarah was riding her 'trusty steed' back to their property when suddenly, her horse tripped, causing Sarah to fall and break her neck.

FATAL ACCIDENT.—Last Friday morning Sarah Alice, daughter of Henry Miller, of the firm of Miller & Lux, was killed at her father's place near Gilroy by her horse falling upon her. She was killed almost instantly.

*Los Angeles Herald, June 18, 1879*

Since then, hundreds of witnesses allege seeing Sarah's ghostly apparition on horseback at Mount Madonna County Park, and some even claim to see her riding in the back seats of their cars.

Sarah is also believed to haunt the Mount Madonna Inn on top of the mountain. Visitors have seen and heard a horse trotting and galloping around the hotel, along with seeing lights turn off and on late at night, when no one was in the building. In recent years, a Park

*The Santa Cruz Ghost Directory*

Ranger claimed to have heard a young woman screaming for help from the Mount Madonna Inn. He searched the perimeter of the building and didn't find anyone.

*Sarah Logan, circa 1879, courtesy of the Gilroy Museum*

*The Santa Cruz Ghost Directory*

Some claim Sarah's father, "The Cattle King," also haunts his beloved land.

*Henry Miller, circa 1880's, public domain photo*

Additional Information:

- In 2010, some campers awoke in the morning at Mount Madonna to find horse tracks and small footprints circling their tent.

MOUNT MADONNA COUNTY PARK
Year established: 1927
7850 Pole Line Road
Watsonville, CA 95076

## Lee Road

Surrounded by a large fence, ancient Costanoan - Ohlone burial grounds sit in a large 7-acre knoll on Lee Road in Watsonville. The burial ground was discovered in 1975, when bones and remains were uncovered while warehouses were going to be built in the vicinity. More remains were found in the same area in 1980.

Once occupied by an Indian village and cemetery over 1,500 years ago, some have claimed to have sighted Ohlone spirits walking along Lee Road, and on the land where their bodies are laid to rest.

Since the property is private, the exact address or region has been restricted.

LEE ROAD
Registered Landmark of Historic Places
Watsonville, CA 95076

## The Redman House

The once beautiful, now run-down Queen Anne Victorian called "The Redman House" resides on Lee Road in the middle of a strawberry field in Watsonville, California. This stately home was designed for James Redman by renowned architect William H. Weeks. In the 1930s, the home was sold to the Hirahara Family who owned the home until 1989. The home has been abandoned ever since. In 1998, locals started The Redman House Committee (now known as the Redman-Hirahara Foundation) to try to save and restore the spooky Victorian with donations from the public.

*The Santa Cruz Ghost Directory*

Amazingly, The Redman is as haunted as it looks. People passing by have sighted and heard the spirits that reside in the home. Some claim to have seen orbs and light anomalies, along with blue and white mists. Legend has it that people were murdered in the house and their angered presence still linger.

*The Redman House*

Many have heard sounds coming from within the Victorian's walls, and mysteriously from way down the road. Doors have been heard slamming shut loudly on their own, and cool, mystifying breezes have been felt coming from the front door, as if it had just slammed shut. Locals also claim to have heard cries for help from various voices from within this old, decrepit house.

Additional Information:
- Several years back, well-known ghost hunter, author, and friend Jeff Dwyer, heard the ghosts of two men arguing behind the front door.

REDMAN HOUSE
Historical Landmark
Year built: 1897
Lee Road at Beach Road
Watsonville, CA 95076

*The Santa Cruz Ghost Directory*

**The Tuttle Mansion**

The big and elegant Victorian was once owned and built for Morris B. Tuttle, his wife, and their 6 children in 1899. Years after the family passed away and left the home, ghost stories began to arise. Disembodied laughter, sounds, and footsteps have been heard within the haunted Tuttle Mansion, in addition to a full-body apparition of a woman ringing an old farm bell.

THE TUTTLE MANSION
Historical landmark
Year built: 1899
723 F East Lake Avenue

*The Santa Cruz Ghost Directory*

Watsonville, CA 95076
(408) 422-3896
www.dustytreasuresantiques.com

### Veteran's Memorial Building

The haunted Veteran's Memorial Building of Watsonville was built in 1934 as a memorial for Veterans and as a social center for the town. For years, many individuals have spoken about their supernatural encounters in this aged structure. Several locals have witnessed a little boy on the show stage dressed in outdated clothing, as well as hear the sounds of a ball bouncing. The stage curtains are said to move mysteriously at random times, as if someone is behind them, but there is never anyone nearby. Visitors have claimed to hear mystifying noises, such as footsteps on the second floor, and the sound of pool balls cracking, yet there are no pool tables in the Veteran's Memorial Building. Objects are said to mysteriously fall off of shelves in the offices, in addition to the sense of being watched.

*The Santa Cruz Ghost Directory*

In 2017, I spoke to a present Veteran's Memorial employee who is a believer. "I have never seen the ghost of the little boy, but we know he's there," he shared with me.

VETERAN'S MEMORIAL BUILDING
Year built: 1934
215 East Beach Street
Watsonville, CA 95076

*The Santa Cruz Ghost Directory*

## MORE HAUNTS

### APTOS
**SEACLIFF STATE BEACH**
State Park Drive
Aptos, CA 95003

**SESNON HOUSE**
Year built: 1858
6500 Soquel Drive
Aptos, CA 95003
(831) 479- 6229

### BEN LOMOND
**HIGHLANDS HOUSE**
Year built: 1930s
Highlands Park
8500 Highway 9
Ben Lomond, CA 95005

*The Santa Cruz Ghost Directory*

## BROOKDALE
### THE BROOKDALE SWIMMING HOLE
San Lorenzo River
Brookdale, CA 95007

## CAPITOLA
### THE CAPITOLA THEATER
Year built: 1948
(Now a parking lot)
120 Monterey Road
Capitola, CA 95010

### MR. TOOT'S COFFEEHOUSE
Year built: 1936
231 Esplanade # 100
Capitola, CA 95010
(831) 475-3679

## FELTON
### FALL CREEK
1400 Felton Empire Road
Felton, CA 95018
(831) 335-4598

*The Santa Cruz Ghost Directory*

**FELTON COVERED BRIDGE**
Historical Landmark
Year built: 1892
Graham Hill Road
Felton, CA 95018

## SANTA CRUZ
**THE BRANCIFORTE PLAZA**
(Once the old Santa Cruz Hospital)
Year built: 1929
555 Soquel Avenue
Santa Cruz, CA 95062

**DELAVEAGA PARK**
Year established: Circa 1908
(At the abandoned zoo)
Prospect Heights
(Between Pacheco Avenue and Elk Street)
Santa Cruz, CA 95062

**LA BAHIA**
Historical Landmark
Year built: 1926

*The Santa Cruz Ghost Directory*

215 Beach Street
Santa Cruz, CA 95060
\*\* PRIVATE RESIDENCES – NO TRESPASSING.

**OAKWOOD CEMETERY**
Year founded: 1908
3301 Paul Sweet Road
Santa Cruz, CA 95065
(831) 475-2464

**PINE KNOLL PET CEMETERY**
Year built: 1934
180 Sims Road
Santa Cruz, CA 95060

**SANTA CRUZ HIGH**
Year founded: 1897
415 Walnut Avenue
Santa Cruz, CA 95060

**SANTA CRUZ MAIN POST OFFICE**
Historical Landmark
Year built: 1912

850 Front Street
Santa Cruz, CA 95060

**SANTA CRUZ TRESTLE (AKA THE LOST BOYS' TRESTLE)**
Historical Landmark
Year built: 1904
Santa Cruz, CA 95060

**THE WATERING HOLE**
Year built: 1949
2405 Mission Street
Santa Cruz, CA 95060
(831) 469-4653

**THE WRIGLEY'S BUILDING**
Year built: 1892
University Business Park
2801 Mission Street
Santa Cruz, CA 95060

**YOGI TEMPLE (AKA COURT OF MYSTERIES)**
Year built: 1930s

519 Fair Street
Santa Cruz, CA 95060
\*\* PRIVATE RESIDENCE- NO TRESPASSING.

## **SOQUEL**
**SOQUEL HIGH**
Year founded: 1962
401 Old San Jose Road
Soquel, CA 95073

## **WATSONVILLE**
**SUNSET STATE BEACH**
201 Sunset Beach Road
Watsonville, CA 95076
(831) 763-7063


\*\* To view the ghost stories of the sites previously listed in this chapter, check out my website at: www.santacruzghostdirectory.com, and my book, **Supernatural Santa Cruz - Second Edition**.

# GLOSSARY

**Cold Spot**: A small, defined area of intense cold that is at least ten degrees colder than the surrounding area, believed to be caused by a ghost when there is no natural or mechanical explanation.

**Conduit**: A person or an object that attracts or draws in spirits for various reasons.

**Dowsing Rods (AKA Divining Rods)**: Two metal, L-shaped rods that move on their own. The dowsing rods have been used for centuries to find rock, graves, water, and any type of solids underneath the Earth. While standing above an area with solid material below, the rods will cross. Paranormal investigators have been using rods for years to communicate with spirits. The entities are able to move the rods for Yes and No responses.

**Ectoplasm**: Spiritual energy that takes form of fluid or mist.

**EMF**: Electromagnetic field

**EVP (Electronic Voice Phenomenon)**: A disembodied voice heard through white noise or on a recorder.

**Flashlight method**: A technique that's used to communicate with spirits by setting a screw-top mini Maglite on a hard surface and asking the spirit(s) to turn the flashlight on and off on command.

**Ghost Radar**: An application you can download on most mobile devices that can detect paranormal activity. It measures electromagnetic fields and identifies energies when they are near. The application also has a built-in Ovilus, which provides a large vocabulary list for spirits to choose from. The app then "speaks" the words chosen.

**K-2 Meter**: A scientific instrument that measures electrometric fields. It is believed that ghosts give off electromagnetic energy which can be picked up on an EMF Detector or K-2 Meter.

**Medium**: A person who is able to channel and communicate with spirits.

**Mel Meter**: A device that measures electromagnetic fields and temperature.

**Orb**: An energy anomaly, normally seen in photographs or on camera, and sometimes witnessed by the naked eye. The circular ball of light has been seen in different colors, and moving in diverse speeds and directions. It is believed to be a spirit in transit.

**Pendulum**: A weight hung by a fixed support that moves under the influence of gravity. Some ghost hunters use pendulums, most commonly made out of a mineral and hung by a string, so that it's easy for spirits to move and manipulate it.

**Residual Energy (or haunting)**: Records of energy that have been imprinted in the area where the (normally traumatic) event took place.

**Vortex**: A doorway or portal to another realm that allows entities and other paranormal phenomena to come into our world.

## SOURCES

Books:
- Beal, Chandra Moira, and Beal, Richard. Santa Cruz Beach Boardwalk: The Early Years - Never a Dull Moment. U.S.A.: The Pacific Group; 2003.
- Browne, Sylvia. Visits from the Afterlife. New York: Penguin Books; 2004.
- Chase, John. The Sidewalk Companion to Santa Cruz Architecture. Santa Cruz, CA: Paper Vision Press; 1979.
- Dennett, Preston. Supernatural California. Pennsylvania: Schiffer Publishing Ltd.; 2006.
- Dwyer, Jeff. Ghost Hunter's Guide to Monterey and California's Central Coast. Gretna, Louisiana: Pelican Publishing Co.; 2010.
- Graves, Aubrey. Supernatural Santa Cruz. Charleston, South Carolina: Createspace; 2011.
- Graves, Aubrey. Supernatural Santa Cruz – Second Edition. Charleston, South Carolina: Createspace; 2013.
- Graves, Aubrey. California Ghost Directory, The. Charleston, South Carolina: Createspace; 2015.
- Koch, Margaret. The Walk Around Santa Cruz Book. Fresno, CA: Valley Publishers; 1978.
- May, Antoinette. Haunted Houses and Wondering Ghosts of California. San Francisco, CA: The SF Examiner division of the Hearst Corporation; 1977.

## *The Santa Cruz Ghost Directory*

•Perry, Frank A; Piwarzyk, Robert W; Luther, Michael D; Orlando, Alverda; Molho, Allan; Perry, Sierra L. <u>Lime Kiln Legacies- The History of the Lime Industry in Santa Cruz County</u>. Santa Cruz: The Museum of Art and History; 2007.

•Reinstedt, Randall A. <u>California Ghost Notes</u>. Carmel, CA: Ghost Town Publications; 2000.

Newspaper Articles:

•Allen-Taylor, Douglas. "Tales of Three Ghosts." Metroactive, 1999.

•Anonymous Author. "A Fatal Accident." Santa Cruz Sentinel, May 15, 1903.

•Anonymous Author. "Another Murder." Santa Cruz Sentinel, August 26, 1890.

•Anonymous Author. "Big Dipper, Truck Fire Accidents Cause Deaths." Santa Cruz Sentinel, July 6, 1958.

•Anonymous Author. "Explosions at the Powder Works Startled This City." Santa Cruz Sentinel, April 27, 1898.

•Anonymous Author. "Frank McLaughlin Kills Daughter and Himself at Santa Cruz." San Francisco Call, November 17, 1907.

•Anonymous Author. "Funeral Rites for Mary Jane Hanly Largely Attended." Santa Cruz Sentinel, September 5, 1937.

•Anonymous Author. "Glamour, gangsters and ghosts: Brookdale Lodge possesses colorful history." Santa Cruz Sentinel, August 19, 2009.

## *The Santa Cruz Ghost Directory*

- Anonymous Author. "Gun Accident Kills Pioneer Family Member." Santa Cruz Sentinel, January 27, 1963.
- Anonymous Author. "Haunted Houses of Santa Cruz." Santa Cruz Sentinel, October 31, 1982.
- Anonymous Author. "His Last Sleep." Santa Cruz Sentinel, October 5, 1884.
- Anonymous Author. "Indian Bones to be Re-Interred." Santa Cruz Sentinel, March 14, 1980.
- Anonymous Author. "Injuries from Fall Fatal to Man." Santa Cruz Sentinel, March 30, 1943.
- Anonymous Author. "Miss Cowell Meets Death in Runaway." San Francisco Call, May 15, 1903.
- Anonymous Author. "Roller Coaster Fall Kills Boy, 13." Santa Cruz Sentinel, July 13, 1972.
- Anonymous Author. "Seaside Company Files Answer to $100, Suit." Santa Cruz Sentinel, July, 1958.
- Anonymous Author. "Several New Clues Appear in Drownings." Santa Cruz Sentinel, June, 1959.
- Anonymous Author. "Terrible Explosions." San Francisco Chronicle, November 9, 1879.
- Anonymous Author. "Walter Fernald Bryne, One of Best Liked and Promising Local Youths Killed in Accident at Beach Dipper." Santa Cruz Evening News, September 22, 1924.
- Anonymous Author. "Youth Drowns in Crowded Beach Plunge." Santa Cruz Evening News, April, 1937.
- Anonymous Author. "Aptos Residents Mourn Death..." Santa Cruz Evening News, September 29, 1928.

## *The Santa Cruz Ghost Directory*

- Anonymous Author. "Best Arts and Entertainment." Good Times, April 25, 2012.
- Anonymous Author. "Psyching Out the Spirits." San Francisco Sunday Examiner & Chronicle, October 30, 1977.
- Asch, Jennifer. "Greetings from Santa Creepy / in and around Santa Cruz, Ghost Stories and Spooky Sites Send Chills Up Visitors' Spines." San Francisco Chronicle, October 31, 1997.
- Baine, Wallace. "A Strange History of a Strange Place." May 29, 2009.
- Basquez, Anna Maria. "Strange Goings-On: McPherson Center, Capitola Theater Join Local 'Haunts'." Santa Cruz Sentinel, October 12, 1998.
- Biasotti, Marianne. "Ohlone Remains Found on PV Site." Santa Cruz Sentinel, May 18, 1994.
- Eng, Julie. "Walking With a Ghost." City on a Hill Press: A student-run newspaper, 2010.
- Gibson, Ross Eric. "Dominican Hospital's Roots Rest with Mystical Mary Jane Hanly." Santa Cruz Sentinel, September 13, 1998.
- Guzman, Isaiah. "Ghostbusters Scour Brookdale Lodge." Santa Cruz Sentinel, January 19, 2008.
- Guzman, Isaiah. "Stirring Up Spirits." Santa Cruz Sentinel, January 11, 2008.
- Harbert, Gregory Jon. "Old Santa Cruz Haunts." Valley Press/ Scotts Valley Banner, 1999.

## *The Santa Cruz Ghost Directory*

- Issacson, Joel. "Old Holy Cross Cemetery Suffers from Vandalism." Santa Cruz Sentinel, December 20, 2008.
- Jacobson, Kate. "Ghost Riding in Santa Cruz." Santa Cruz Weekly, October 28, 2010.
- Kimura, Donna. "A Crime Scene That's as Cold as the Grave." Santa Cruz Sentinel, August 1, 1996.
- Koch, Margaret. "Ghost Stories: Bizarre Tales Haunt Local History." Santa Cruz Sentinel, January 22, 1991.
- Lawshe, Mark. "Ghost Story of Sarah Cowell." Santa Cruz Sentinel, October 30, 1975.
- Lawshe, Mark. "Goblins, Ghosts in the Area." Santa Cruz Sentinel, October 29, 1975.
- Leal, Carolyn. "Soquel Sentinel." Santa Cruz Sentinel, April 13, 2003.
- Martin, Christa. "Visiting Some of Our Favorite Haunts." Good Times, October 19, 2000.
- Mickelson, Gwen. "Fabled Brookdale Lodge - - Ghost and all - - Up for Sale." Santa Cruz Sentinel, May 17, 2007.
- Miller, Donald. "A Haunted Clubhouse?" Santa Cruz Sentinel, December 12, 1988.
- Morgan, Terri. "A Halloween Tale: The Curse of Pogonip." Santa Cruz Sentinel, October 31, 2006.
- Musitelli, Robin. "Ghostly Goings on at Haunted Houses." Santa Cruz Sentinel, October 27, 1996.
- Orion, Damon. "Surreal Estate." Good Times, June 10, 1999.
- Parker, Ann. "Spirited Dining at the Brookdale Lodge." Santa Cruz Sentinel, September 14, 2005.

## *The Santa Cruz Ghost Directory*

- Parker, Ann. "Spirited goings-on at Scottish Pub." Santa Cruz Sentinel, May 14, 2006.
- Phelan, Sarah. "Hex Appeal." Metro Santa Cruz, September 6, 2002.
- Phelan, Sarah. "The Ghost Stays in the Picture." Metro Santa Cruz, October 9, 2002.
- Phelan, Sarah. "The Haunting of Santa Cruz." Metro Santa Cruz, October 29, 2003.
- Righetti, Don. "Mark Abbott Lighthouse Dedication." Santa Cruz Sentinel, November 22, 1967.
- Robinson, John. "Ghosts Said to Haunt Hotel." Santa Cruz Sentinel, October 31, 1986.
- Rogers, Paul. "Dislodging the Ghosts? Eerie Events at Hotel Rattle Owners, Lead top Exorcism." Mercury News, January 4, 1991.
- Seals, Brian. "La Conchita Mudslide Stirs Memories of Love Creek Catastrophe." Santa Cruz Sentinel, January 13, 2005.
- Spicuzza, Mary. "Santa Cruz Suburban Legends." Metro Santa Cruz, 1999.
- Swift, Carolyn. "Rispin is a Setting Worthy of the Spirit World." Santa Cruz Sentinel, October 31, 1999.
- Townsend, Peggy. "Ghost Stories: Voices, Ghouls and a Love That Lasts Forever." Santa Cruz Sentinel, October 31, 2004.
- Trabing, Wally. "Old Santa Cruz Ghost Story." Santa Cruz Sentinel, January 30, 1975.

## *The Santa Cruz Ghost Directory*

- Tryde, Wendy. "Ghosts of an Old Hotel." Santa Cruz Sentinel, October 31, 2000.
- Unknown (Anonymous) "Fact or Fright Fiction." Morgan Hill Times, October 28, 2005.
- Walch, Bob. "Brookdale Lodge's Ghost Intrigues Tourists." Santa Cruz Sentinel, October 25, 2007.

Web:

- http://backpackerverse.com/beach-camping-northern-california/#5_Seacliff_State_Beach_8211_Aptos
- http://backpackerverse.com/best-beaches-in-california/
- http://coursetrained.blogspot.com/2008/08/lost-tunnels-los-gatos-to-santa-cruz.html
- http://darkhaunts.com/CaliforniaGhostStoryIndexPAGE2.html
- http://ediblemontereybay.com/blog/is-cremer-house-haunted/
- http://en.allexperts.com/q/California-89/f/Mount-Madonna.htm
- http://en.wikipedia.org/wiki/Alfred_Hitchcock
- http://en.wikipedia.org/wiki/California_State_Route_17
- http://en.wikipedia.org/wiki/Talk%3ALimestone#Limestone_in_haunted_locations.3F.3F.3F
- http://ghost-girls.org/

http://gocalifornia.about.com/od/camissions/ss/mission-santa-cruz_2.htm

- http://hilltromper.com/article/horrors-summit-tunnel

## The Santa Cruz Ghost Directory

- http://kfrc.radio.com/2010/10/25/bay-areas-most-haunted-places/
- http://naturalplane.blogspot.com/2011/04/bobo-enigma-of-monterey-bay.html?utm_source=feedburner&utm_medium=feed&utm_campaign=Feed%3A+PhantomsAndMonstersAPersonalJourney+(Phantoms+and+Monsters)
- http://researchforum.santacruzmah.org/viewtopic.php?t=75&view=next&sid=5c95bf280c0cf5e180547c751854a55f
- http://researchforum.santacruzmah.org/viewtopic.php?t=83
- http://santacruzparanormalresearch.blogspot.com/2009/02/partial-catalog-of-haunted-places-in-sc.html
- http://scplweb.santacruzpl.org/history/spanish/kimholy.shtml
- http://sluggosghoststories.blogspot.com/2009/05/porter-college-university-of-california.html
- http://sluggosghoststories.blogspot.com/2009/06/white-lady-of-graham-hill-road.html
- http://theshadowlands.net
- http://www.angelfire.com
- http://www.athanasius.com/camission/cruz.htm
- http://www.bigfootdiscoveryproject.com/
- http://www.capitolamuseum.org/1930rispin.html
- http://www.carpenoctem.tv/haunt/ca/
- http://www.cityonahillpress.com/2010/11/18/walking-with-a-ghost/
- http://www.cliffcrestinn.com/

## The Santa Cruz Ghost Directory

- http://www.costaricantimes.com/exploring-the-supernatural-in-santa-cruz-california/30246
- http://www.examiner.com/arizona-haunted-sites-in-phoenix/arizona-ghost-hunter-travels-roaring-camp-railroad-ghost
- http://www.ghostsofamerica.com
- http://www.ghoststudy.com/ghost%20stories/sep00/santacruz.html
- http://www.hauntedbay.com
- http://www.hauntedhouses.com/states/ca/
- http://www.hauntedplaces.org/item/surf-bistro-and-bakery/
- http://www.legendsofamerica.com/ca-hauntedhotels3.html
- http://www.liparanormalinvestigators.com/rocks.shtml
- http://www.mcpost.com/article.php?id=773
- http://www.mnn.net/roarhike.htm
- http://www.mobileranger.com/santacruz/the-cremer-house-scandalous-stories-from-feltons-oldest-building/
- http://www.montereycountyweekly.com/news/2007/oct/25/monster-swell/
- http://www.npr.org/programs/lnfsound/scrapbook/kitchensisters.html

http://www.redmanhouse.com/history.shtml

- http://www.roaringcamp.com/pdfs/RoaringCampHistory.pdf
- http://www.santacruzpl.org/history/articles/183/
- http://www.santacruzpl.org/history/articles/427/

## *The Santa Cruz Ghost Directory*

- http://www.santacruzpl.org/history/articles/446/
- http://www.santacruzsentinel.com/ci_15163347
- http://www.scparks.com/highlands.html
- http://www.scparks.com/Home/RecreationPrograms/QuailHollowRanch%E2%80%93InterpretivePrograms/CulturalHistory.aspx
- http://www.scparks.com/Portals/12/pdfs/QHR_a_History.pdf
- http://www.seabreezetavern.com/history.html
- http://www.shadowbrook-capitola.com/
- http://www.strangeusa.com
- http://www.svchamber.org/svhistory/history/hitchcock.htm
- http://www.thecobrasnose.com/xxghost/santacruz.html
- http://www.ufostalker.com/event/73386
- http://www.unexplainable.net/artman/publish/article_14552.shtml
- http://www.valleyhaunts.net/showthread.php?tid=88
- http://www.vaughns-1-pagers.com/history/rispin-mansion.htm
- http://www.yourghoststories.com/real-ghost-story.php?story=879
- http://www3.gendisasters.com/california/15542/big-tree-ca-train-wrecked-may-1880?page=0%2C0
- https://localwiki.org/santacruz/Lady_of_the_Sea
- https://www.youtube.com/watch?v=wg8MpBKLxhs
- www.charlespeden.wordpress.com

# BOOKS BY AUBREY GRAVES

*Supernatural Santa Cruz*, 2011

*Ghosts of Santa Clara County*, 2012

*The Unofficial Guide to Disneyland's Haunted Kingdom*, 2012

*Supernatural Santa Cruz - Second Edition*, 2013

*ATTACHMENT: A Santa Cruz Ghost Story*, 2013

*The Haunted Brookdale Lodge*, 2014

*The California Ghost Directory*, 2014

*The History of the Brookdale Lodge*, 2017

- Books are available for purchase on Amazon.com.

## ABOUT THE AUTHOR

Paranormal investigator and empath Aubrey Graves resides in Santa Cruz, California with her loved ones, both living and dead.

*The Santa Cruz Ghost Directory*

Aubrey grew up in a haunted house and has always had a vast interest in the supernatural. She has been collecting ghost stories told around Santa Cruz since 2007, and published her first book, *Supernatural Santa Cruz* in 2011.

Had a paranormal experience in Santa Cruz County that you'd like to share? Please write to:
aubreygraves@hotmail.com

**www.santacruzghostdirectory.com**

Made in the USA
Coppell, TX
22 April 2022